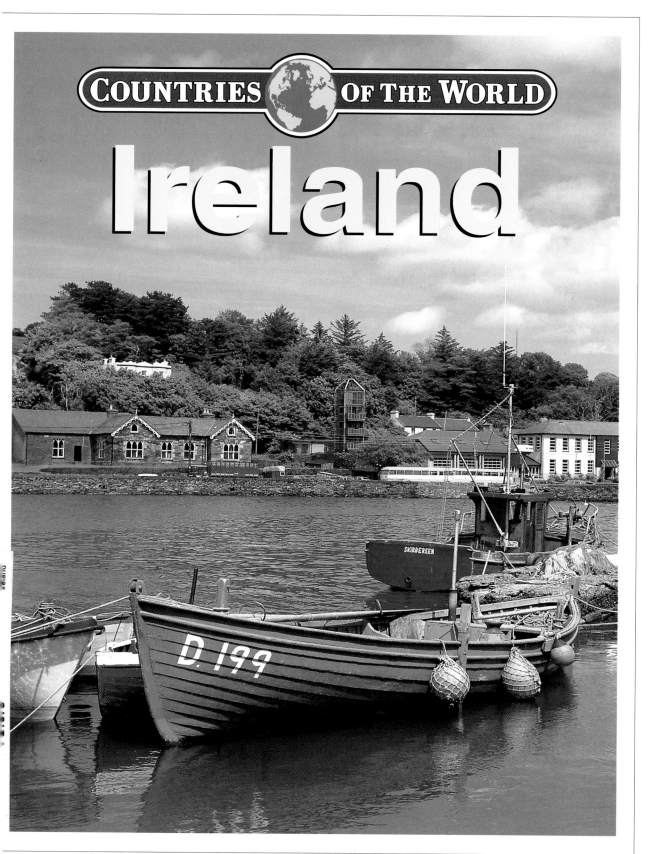

COUNTRIES OF THE WORLD

Ireland

Gareth Stevens Publishing
MILWAUKEE

About the Author: Shannon Spencer is currently a doctoral candidate at Yale University's School of Forestry and Environmental Studies. She has written numerous papers on development-related issues and has been a teaching assistant for several graduate level courses. She has visited Ireland twice, spending time primarily in the Dublin area, on the west coast, and in County Donegal, in the northwestern part of the island.

Written by
SHANNON SPENCER

Edited by
GERALDINE MESENAS

Designed by
JAILANI BASARI

Picture research by
SUSAN JANE MANUEL

First published in North America in 2000 by
Gareth Stevens Publishing
1555 North RiverCenter Drive, Suite 201
Milwaukee, Wisconsin 53212 USA

For a free color catalog describing
Gareth Stevens' list of high-quality books
and multimedia programs, call
1-800-542-2595 (USA) or
1-800-461-9120 (CANADA).
Gareth Stevens Publishing's
Fax: (414) 225-0377.

© **TIMES EDITIONS PTE LTD 2000**
Originated and designed by
Times Editions Pte Ltd
Times Centre, 1 New Industrial Road
Singapore 536196
http://www.timesone.com.sg/te

Library of Congress Cataloging-in-Publication Data
Spencer, Shannon.
Ireland / by Shannon Spencer.
p. cm. — (Countries of the world)
Includes bibliographical references and index.
Summary: An overview of Ireland which provides information on its geography, history, government, lifestyles, language, art, food, and current issues.
ISBN 0-8368-2318-4 (lib. bdg.)
1. Ireland—Juvenile literature. [1. Ireland.] I. Title. II. Series: Countries of the world (Milwaukee, Wis.)
DA906.S64   2000
941.7—dc21   99-36636

Printed in Malaysia

1 2 3 4 5 6 7 8 9 04 03 02 01 00

PICTURE CREDITS
A.N.A. Press Agency: 3 (center), 9 (top), 36
Archive Photos: 15 (top), 15 (center), 16, 29 (bottom, left), 46, 59 (right), 61, 79, 80, 85 (both)
Holzbachova Benet: 4, 11, 13, 24, 26, 33, 35, 37, 39, 47, 69 (both), 78, 81
Bes Stock: 87
Michele Burgess: 41
Jan Butchofsky: 34, 50, 64
Focus Team: 3 (bottom), 20, 25, 27, 28, 30, 38, 40 (both), 51, 60
Blaine Harrington: 19, 29 (top), 32 (bottom), 44, 71, 75, 83 (bottom), 91
HBL Network: 14
Ingrid Horstman: 22
Dave G. Houser: 10, 70
The Hutchison Library: 7, 17, 18, 66
International Photobank: Cover, 1, 2, 6, 53, 74
North Wind Picture Archives: 52, 55, 63, 68, 72, 73, 76
Topham Picturepoint: 12, 15 (bottom), 21, 29 (bottom, right), 31, 32 (top), 54, 56, 57, 58, 59 (left), 67, 77, 82, 83 (top), 84
Travel Ink: 42, 43, 45
Trip Photographic Library: 3 (top), 8, 9 (bottom), 23, 48, 49 (both), 62, 65, 89

Digital Scanning by Superskill Graphics Pte Ltd

Contents

AN OVERVIEW OF IRELAND

Often associated with leprechauns and lucky charms, Ireland is a small island nation with warm, welcoming people and an enchanting landscape. Irish history is filled with clashes between different groups of people, but, today, Ireland is mostly a land where cattle roam and people live peacefully together, socializing and talking. Music and storytelling are two favorite Irish pastimes, and no wonder — the people of Ireland have some of the sharpest wits and most vivid imaginations in the world.

The history of Ireland has been tumultuous; the Irish have endured centuries of exploitation by the British. In the nineteenth century, millions of Irish emigrated to the United States and other countries to escape famine and poverty. Today, however, more young Irish are remaining in their home country, boosting its economy and keeping its rich cultural traditions alive. The island remains divided between Northern Ireland (part of the United Kingdom), which has a Protestant majority, and the Republic of Ireland, a Catholic stronghold. Both sides have maintained a cease-fire since 1994.

Opposite: **Built in 1446, Blarney Castle now stands in ruins. Tourists come from all over the world to see the famous Blarney Stone, said to confer the gift of eloquence on all who kiss it.**

THE FLAG OF THE REPUBLIC OF IRELAND

The flag of the Republic of Ireland has three vertical panels of green, white, and orange. The green band represents Catholics of native Irish descent; the orange band, descendants of the seventeenth-century British Protestants (a group of people who supported England's King William of Orange); and the white band, hope for peace between these two groups. The Irish tricolor, as the flag is called, was not adopted as the national flag until after the Easter Rising of 1916, when 2,500 Irish rebelled against British rule in Dublin.

THE FLAG OF NORTHERN IRELAND

The flag of Northern Ireland is based on the flag of England, with the red cross of Saint George, the patron saint of England, in the background. The red hand is derived from the legend of a war party leader who promised a prize to the first man to touch land with his right hand. Hearing this, a left-handed man cut off his right hand and flung it to the shore, winning the challenge. The six points of the star refer to the six counties of Ulster that make up Northern Ireland. This flag has been used as a banner of arms by the government of Northern Ireland since 1925, but it was not officially adopted until 1953.

Geography

Physical Environment

Ireland sits directly west of Great Britain, across the Irish Sea. The small island of 27,136 square miles (70,283 square kilometers) is divided between the Republic of Ireland, which covers about 85 percent of the land, and Northern Ireland. Ireland's landscape is remarkably varied, ranging from the rugged cliffs, rocky promontories, and inlets of the western coast to the rolling hills and wetlands of the central lowlands. There is little natural woodland left in Ireland, and a large part of the country consists of pasture, which is used mainly for farming and grazing cattle. The longest river in Ireland is the River Shannon, and the largest lakes on the island are Lough Neagh in Northern Ireland and Lough Ree in the Republic of Ireland. The Blue Stack Mountains in County Donegal and the Caha Mountains in Counties Kerry and Cork form Ireland's main mountain ranges.

Most of the roads in the Irish countryside are narrow and lined on both sides by stone walls that serve several functions. Since Irish soil is filled with rocks, stone walls have always been

THE ARAN ISLANDS

Crisscrossed by dry stone walls and dotted with prehistoric ring forts, the Aran Islands (Inishmore, Inishmaan, and Inisheer) have retained many traditions, notably Aran knitwear.
(A Closer Look, page 44)

Below: **Bantry Bay in County Cork is a large, deep-water inlet and a natural harbor.**

the least expensive and most practical way of marking boundaries between lands belonging to different people or between lands that have different uses. Stone walls are also used to confine herd animals so they do not stray.

Above: **Dublin is the business and political center of the Republic of Ireland. The River Liffey cuts through the center of the city, and some of Dublin's most important buildings sit along its banks.**

Dublin

The majority of people in the Republic of Ireland live on the eastern coast, especially in or near Dublin, the Irish capital and the center of the Irish government. About 600,000 people live within the city limits, and about one million people inhabit the entire metropolitan area. Dublin is famous for its small streets and elegant public buildings. The city's beautiful architecture and its proximity to England contribute to its popularity among both tourists and locals. As a result, development pressure on Ireland's eastern coast is centered around Dublin and its surrounding areas. Over decades, highways, residential housing projects, and modern shopping malls have been built to meet the needs of the growing population.

Seasons

The Irish landscape is covered with brilliant green grass, earning Ireland its nickname, *The Emerald Isle.* Grass and plants stay green even during winter because of the temperate climate and the abundance of rain.

Ireland's mild climate is created by southwesterly wind currents that pull warm air up from the Gulf of Mexico and over the Atlantic Ocean, sending it across the Irish landscape. The temperatures in summer range from 40° to 70° Fahrenheit (4.4° to 21.1° Celsius). Winter temperatures are mild, ranging from 30° to 40° F (-1.1° to 4.4° C). Mountainous regions, however, experience extremely harsh winters.

Plentiful rainfall keeps Ireland's plant life green year-round. Western Ireland, which faces the Atlantic, is the wettest region on the island, while the southeastern parts are the driest. The average amount of rainfall varies very little throughout the year. During spring and summer, the driest seasons, average rainfall is about 2 inches (51 millimeters) per month. Rainfall averages about 3 inches (76 mm) per month during autumn and winter, the wettest seasons. Weather forecasts in Ireland typically predict that any given day will be partly sunny, with a chance of showers and moderate temperatures.

Above: **Lush green grass is the hallmark of the Emerald Isle.**

Plants

The widest diversity of plant life is found on Ireland's largely undeveloped western coast, where the climate is suitably wet. Plants found in Ireland include the thrift, water lobelia, Kerry lily, sea campion, bog asphodel, meadow vetchling, and sundew plant.

Animals

Ireland is well-known for an absence of snakes. Legend has it that Saint Patrick, the patron saint of Ireland, banished them from the island. Common native species include gray seals, which feed off the Atlantic coast; pine martens, which are nocturnal animals of the weasel family; and otters, also called "river dogs," which can be seen in the shallow waters off rocky coasts and, occasionally, in rivers and streams.

Above: **Famous for its brightly colored beak and expressionless face, the puffin is one of Ireland's more unusual birds.**

A Bird-Lover's Paradise

Many different kinds of birds live in Ireland, particularly on the island's western coast, a prime bird-watching area and a popular stop for birds en route to other habitats. One bird that nests on Ireland's western coast is the puffin, notable for its unusual markings. The undisturbed coastal setting is also a haven for threatened bird species, such as the corncrake.

Left: **Alpine goldenrod peeks through cracks in the Burren.**

THE BURREN

A vast limestone plateau in County Clare, the Burren supports a unique range of flora and fauna, from Mediterranean plants to Whooper swans.

(A Closer Look, page 48)

9

History

Early History

In about the sixth century B.C., Ireland was invaded by the *Celts* (KELTZ), also known as the *Gaels* (GAYLZ), who came from the European mainland. They conquered the Firbolg, a native Irish people about whom little is known. Celtic civilization survived for centuries in Ireland despite Christianization and trade with mainland Europe. The Roman Empire occupied Britain for four hundred years but never reached Irish shores, thus ensuring that Ireland would maintain a different character from the rest of Britain.

Over the following centuries, Ireland was invaded by Norsemen, Normans (who came from Europe), and the English, and the country was bedeviled with civil wars that often did more harm to the Irish than did the foreign invaders.

In the twelfth century, King Henry II of England laid claim to Ireland. The distance, however, from England to Ireland made English rule difficult and largely limited it to an area around the city of Dublin, known as "the Pale."

VIKINGS IN DUBLIN

The Vikings invaded Celtic Ireland in the later part of the eighth century and founded Dublin in 841. It was not until the 1970s that ancient Viking relics were discovered in the Irish capital.
(*A Closer Look, page 72*)

Below: **Built some time between the sixth and ninth centuries, Gallarus Oratory, located on the Dingle Peninsula, is one of the oldest churches in Ireland.**

English Rule

Gaelic society consisted of a loose association of tribes that shared laws, customs, and language under the symbolic leadership of a High King, who ruled from a place called the Hill of Tara. The complicated clash of Gaelic traditions and English laws enforced by King Henry VIII of England brought about the downfall of the tribal system that had existed in Ireland for hundreds of years. As Gaelic leaders were deposed, English leaders took over claims to the land, which was then settled by the English. This brought about an important change — Ireland's population had previously been largely Catholic, but now, the newly Protestant English, under Henry VIII, were gaining a foothold.

At this time in Irish history, religion, rather than national origin, determined the political scene. Catholics were instantly opposed to Protestants. There was also general discontent among the Irish at having lost their Gaelic traditions, but no coordinated political uprising challenged the new system of English rule for several more centuries. Although rebellions were periodically staged against allegedly unfair English practices, these uprisings were put down through the Penal Laws, which largely removed all social rights from Catholics, including the right to own or lease land.

Above: **Irish clan leader Thomas Fitzgerald renounced his allegiance to King Henry VIII in 1534 and was hanged in 1537. Like Fitzgerald, many Irish Catholics were outraged when Henry VIII created the Church of England and made it England's official religion over Catholicism. Henry's assumption of the title** *King of Ireland* **also angered them.**

CASTLES IN IRELAND

Ireland's historic charm is most visible in the many stone castles that guard the countryside. Today, some of these architectural wonders have been restored and given a new lease on life as tourist attractions.

(A Closer Look, page 50)

11

Left: **The Easter Rising of 1916 triggered civil wars between Protestant and Catholic militant groups in Northern Ireland.**

The Penal Laws

The Penal Laws largely legislated Irish Catholics into the peasant class. The Irish parliament was also disbanded, and Ireland was legislatively united with Britain. After the Penal Laws were implemented, Irish peasants lived in extreme poverty, while their landlords extorted extremely high rents from them. The Penal Laws were repealed in 1778 and 1872.

The mid-1800s brought Irish leader Daniel O'Connell to center stage in Irish politics, and with him came a new political sense of Ireland as a nation. He rallied national support, first for the emancipation of the Catholics, and then, for the repeal of the legal union between England and Ireland. The Great Famine, however, of 1845 to 1848, dwarfed political developments.

Political Change

In 1905, nationalist leader Arthur Griffith founded the Irish Catholic group Sinn Fein, which became the most influential nationalist group in Ireland. Home rule was enacted in 1914, with the provision that Ulster (now Northern Ireland) should remain in the union for six more years. This act, however, was suspended during World War I and was never put into effect. In 1916, the Easter Rising was organized against British rule. The uprising failed but received great attention when the British executed some if its leaders. The rebellion was linked to Sinn Fein and contributed to the group's landslide

THE GREAT FAMINE

During the mid-1800s, a blight wiped out Ireland's potato crop, the staple food of Irish peasants. As a result, over one million people died of disease and starvation. Mass emigrations took place during the period 1847–1854.

(A Closer Look, page 54)

victory in the British parliamentary elections of 1918. The newly elected Sinn Fein parliamentary members, led by a surviving leader of the Easter Rising, Eamon de Valera, refused to take their seats in London's Westminster Abbey. Instead, they declared themselves the Dail Eireann (Irish Assembly), proclaiming an Irish republic. The British outlawed both Sinn Fein and the Dail. The Irish Republican Army (IRA) was organized to resist British authority and fight for recognition of the Irish republic. The IRA waged a guerrilla war against local Irish authorities who represented the British-Irish union. The British responded by sending troops, called the Black and Tans for their distinctive uniforms, that used severe tactics to crush the IRA.

A Country Divided

In 1920, a new home rule bill was enacted, establishing separate parliaments for Ulster (Northern Ireland) and Catholic Ireland (southern Ireland). This bill, accepted by Ulster, created Northern Ireland. In 1922, southern Ireland became the Irish Free State, a dominion of the United Kingdom. De Valera was made the Irish prime minister in 1932, and a new constitution established the sovereign nation of Ireland, or Eire, within the British Commonwealth of Nations. De Valera aimed his policies at political and economic independence from Britain.

Below: The Irish peace delegation and the ministers of the Dail met in 1921. The Dail rejected the home rule bill of 1920, but in the autumn of 1921, a treaty was signed, granting dominion status to Catholic Ireland within the United Kingdom. The Irish Free State was established in January, 1922, after which civil war broke out between its supporters and those who opposed maintaining ties with Britain.

The Republic of Ireland

De Valera proclaimed the Republic of Ireland on April 18, 1949, withdrawing Ireland from the British Commonwealth entirely and formally claiming jurisdiction over Northern Ireland. There was no response to the claim until the late 1960s, when fighting broke out between the Protestant majority and the Catholic minority in Northern Ireland. The fighting was spurred on by the IRA, which continued its guerilla warfare in a quest to end the union between Northern Ireland and Great Britain. Fighting has continued off and on over the decades. A number of peace agreements have been made and then broken. The most recent peace accord, still in effect, was arrived at in April, 1998, and was approved by popular vote in both Northern Ireland and in the Irish Republic.

Since the 1960s, the Republic of Ireland has made considerable social and economic progress, although unemployment remains a challenge today. The government's social policies, which included relaxing laws on contraception in the 1980s, have met with mixed reactions from the Catholic population and concern from the Roman Catholic Church.

THE HISTORY OF "THE TROUBLES"

Clashes between Irish Catholics and Protestants in Northern Ireland have resulted in many deaths and the destruction of property. In 1998, the Good Friday Peace Agreement was signed between Irish Catholic and Protestant militant groups. This agreement could be an important first step toward eventual peace in Northern Ireland. *(A Closer Look, page 56)*

Left: **The leader of Sinn Fein, Gerry Adams, talks to supporters in Northern Ireland.**

Daniel O'Connell (1775–1847)

One of the founders of the Catholic Association in 1823, Daniel O'Connell was known as "the Liberator" for his leadership in the Irish fight for Catholic emancipation from English rule. In 1828, O'Connell was elected to a seat in the House of Commons, but because he was Catholic, he was unable to take the oath required to sit in the British parliament. In 1829, the British government was obliged to pass the Catholic Emancipation Act, and O'Connell took his rightful place in parliament. There, he continued to work for the reformation of the Irish government and to end compulsory support for the Protestant Church of Ireland. In 1841, he became the first Catholic Lord Mayor of Dublin since the thirteenth century.

Daniel O'Connell

Eamon de Valera (1882–1975)

Born in the United States, Eamon de Valera came to Ireland as a child. He took part in the Easter Rising of 1916 and was sentenced to life imprisonment, but he was released under a general amnesty in 1917. That same year, de Valera was elected both to the British parliament and to the presidency of Sinn Fein. In 1919, he was arrested again but escaped and fled to the United States. While abroad, de Valera was elected president of Ireland by the Dail Eireann. He returned to Ireland in the 1920s and became prime minister of the Irish Free State from 1932 to 1948, serving two further terms — from 1951 to 1954 and from 1957 to 1959. In 1959, he became president of the Republic of Ireland, an office he held until 1973.

Eamon de Valera

Mary Robinson (1944–)

Mary Robinson's career began at the age twenty-five, when she became the youngest ever professor of law at Trinity College, Dublin. She went on to spend twenty years as a barrister and as a senator in the Irish parliament. In 1990, Robinson ran for the presidency as an independent candidate backed by the Labour Party. She was elected and used the position to direct attention to social issues. In addition to the ideals she brought to the presidency, the fact that she is a practicing Catholic married to a Protestant provided a role model for a liberal and civic morality distinct from old-style Catholicism.

Mary Robinson

Government and the Economy

System of Government

The Republic of Ireland is a representative democracy. It is governed by a prime minister, a cabinet, and a two-chamber parliamentary legislature. The parliament, or Oireachtas, meets in Dublin. Its two chambers are the Dail Eireann, or the Irish Assembly, and the Seanad Eireann, or the Irish Senate. The Dail is the more powerful chamber, and its 166 members are elected directly by the public. The sixty members of the Seanad are either appointed or elected. The parliament has the sole and exclusive power to make laws, but only the Dail can initiate bills to amend the constitution or propose financial legislation, called Money Bills.

Left: **In 1998, the current Irish president, Mary McAleese, spoke at Harvard University, in the United States, addressing freedom of speech and victims' rights.**

Above: **The imposing facade of City Hall in Belfast, Northern Ireland.**

The Dail and the Seanad work together to create laws, and each house has the power to form committees for specific purposes. Recent committees have addressed issues such as foreign affairs, the Irish language, women's rights, family matters, and sustainable development.

The prime minister presides over parliament and is the most powerful person in the Irish government. The Dail nominates a candidate for prime minister, who is then appointed by the president. The current prime minister, or *Taoiseach* (TEE-shock), is Bertie Ahern. Cabinet members serve in specific areas, such as justice, education, agriculture, defense, trade, finance, and social affairs.

The Irish president serves a seven-year term and is elected by popular vote. As the guardian of the constitution, the president signs bills into law and has the right to address the joint Houses of Parliament. In practice, however, the president does not influence government policy. No Irish president may serve more than two terms. The current Irish president is Mary McAleese.

Economy

The Irish economy has undergone substantial changes since the 1970s. In Northern Ireland, "the Troubles" (the period of political strife between Catholics and Protestants) has slowed down heavy industries and discouraged new investors. In the Republic, however, tax incentives have attracted many multinational firms, especially computing and chemical companies. As a result, the economy has improved substantially, living standards have gone up, and many rural workers have moved to towns where there are better-paying jobs. Multinational companies also account for many of Ireland's exports, but, because they are owned by parent companies in other countries, the profits tend to return to their home countries rather than be invested in the Irish economy.

Agriculture, particularly cattle ranching, and fishing are very important to the Irish economy, and both contribute substantially to the economy. Tourism is increasing, with more than three million visitors arriving in the Republic each year. Yet, due to historical as well as physical factors, the Irish economy is still weak compared to other countries in the European Union (EU). British colonizers exploited Irish farmland but did little else to boost the economy. Most of the industry that the British did bring

TEXTILES OF IRELAND

The Irish textile industry plays an important part in Ireland's economy. Irish textiles and knitwear, such as Donegal tweed, Aran sweaters, and Irish linen, are world famous.
(*A Closer Look, page 70*)

Below: **Agriculture remains one of the most important sectors of the Irish economy.**

Left: These fishermen take pains to clean their vessel before the next trip.

to the island was located in Northern Ireland and, therefore, was lost to the Republic when it separated from the north. Ireland also lacks natural resources, especially fossil fuels, which it imports. Although farmland is plentiful, the soil is so stony that farmers have a hard time making good profits. In addition to these factors, many of Ireland's best and brightest citizens have emigrated to other countries in search of better jobs, higher pay, and bigger opportunities. Finally, Ireland's reputation as an "offshore island of an offshore island" is not particularly attractive to companies. Nevertheless, Ireland's favorable tax environment and its hardworking, well-educated workforce have proven to be good incentives for businesses.

Many Irish workers are employed in small businesses, the service industry, or agriculture. A growing number are employed by large multinational companies. Despite these successes, Ireland has a very high unemployment rate — over 8 percent in January 1999.

Traveling in Ireland

The Irish road and public transportation system is extensive. An excellent bus system serves even remote areas of the island, and, although trains run primarily to the larger towns, the railroad system serves the entire country.

PEATLAND

Peat was traditionally used for fuel in Ireland. Today, however, peat burning is prohibited in many parts of the country because it contributes to air pollution. Irish authorities also wish to conserve the island's remaining peatland.

(A Closer Look, page 66)

People and Lifestyle

For many centuries, ancient Irish peoples, Celts, Norsemen, Normans, and English have intermingled, resulting in an Irish population today that is remarkably homogenous in its ethnic makeup. Most Irish can trace their lineage to one or more of the early groups of people. In the nineteenth century, many Irish fled the poverty that plagued the country during and after the Great Famine of 1845–1848. They emigrated to countries such as England, Canada, and the United States. In recent years, many people have immigrated to Ireland from other parts of the world, but their numbers are limited. In the Republic, about 50 percent of the population is under the age of twenty-five, which may signify improvements in the Irish economy, as well as a renewed interest in living in Ireland rather than emigrating to other countries.

The Irish Lifestyle

The Irish are generally known to be honest, hardworking people. In urban areas, they tend to be modern in their daily routines. Many Dubliners, for example, commute, or ride trains, to work from the suburbs where they live. They usually work at desk jobs

Left: **Many Irish today have mixed Celtic, Norse, Norman, or English ancestry.**

or in the tourist industry, and, at the end of the working day, they might stop at a pub in the city to socialize and have a mug of beer before heading back home on the train.

Rural Irish, particularly farmers, tend to be more traditional in their routines. Many workers on small farms get up early to do chores and tend the animals. In the evening, they might go to the local pub to get together with friends.

The extremes of wealth and poverty are not as far apart in Ireland as in some countries, although there are people who fall into both categories. Among the poorest are a group of people called the Travelers, who live by roadsides and carry all their belongings with them. Their wandering lifestyle resembles that of traditional Gypsies. At the other end of the spectrum are the extremely wealthy, many of whom live in Dublin and travel the world rather than the back roads of Ireland.

Family Life

Family life is very important to the Irish, and it is, in some ways, influenced by the role of the Catholic Church. Divorce is discouraged by the Church and, until the mid-1980s, it was illegal in Ireland, so many couples remained married in name only, since they had no other choice. Catholicism also disallows contraception. Practicing Catholics are therefore more likely to have the bigger families.

Children are well-loved in Ireland and are included in many adult social events, such as dinner parties, concerts, and dance performances. Many adult gathering places, including pubs, also admit children — particularly places in less urbanized areas. Irish families are often tightly knit, participating together in social and church activities.

Prompted by the poor local economy and the lure of prospects abroad, many young Irish travel to other countries for at least part of their lives. There, they work and learn skills they can bring back to Ireland and start businesses with, although many of them end up staying in their adopted homelands. The United States and Canada are popular destinations, and increasing numbers of young Irish are spending time in Europe, also.

Above: **Irish weddings are often elaborate, expensive events.**

Housing and Modernization

Although there are many modern houses in Ireland, many families still live in smaller, more traditional homes. These houses are often single-story structures made of stone and plaster, with thatched roofs. Some small villages still look much like they did before modern technology became such a powerful presence on the eastern coast of Ireland. Even these communities, however, are under increasing pressure to modernize.

Left: **These apartments in Dublin are relatively inexpensive. There are very few high-rise projects in Ireland, because high-rise housing is unpopular.**

Education

The Irish people are generally well-educated. Literacy and secondary school graduation rates are high — almost 80 percent. This phenomenon is most likely a legacy of past times, when Irish peasants saw self-improvement as a way of escaping poverty.

Public schools are supervised and partly paid for by the state, but they have long been run by the Catholic Church, the Protestant Church, or other local organizations. Today, the dominance of religion in education is waning as teachers, administrators, and school board members are increasingly drawn from people not associated with the Church. The government plans to continue this secularization of education. Although the state currently sets the curriculum, most parents in rural Ireland still prefer to have their children receive a Christian-based education.

In School

Irish students study history, English, mathematics, Gaelic (GAY-lik), foreign languages, and other subjects. Academic

Below: **Schools often organize day trips or excursions to popular sights, such as the eighteenth-century Bantry House in southern Ireland, near Cork.**

achievements are emphasized over technical skills, although this is slowly changing. To graduate from secondary school, students must pass tests in five to seven subjects that usually include Gaelic, history, mathematics, and a foreign language.

Extracurricular activities include music, riding lessons, and instruction in traditional Irish dancing, called step dancing. Young people are sometimes expected to help out with the family farm or business, particularly in rural areas of Ireland. Singing is a favorite Irish pastime, as is shopping, spending time with friends, or playing sports, such as soccer or Gaelic football.

Above: **Trinity College in Dublin has, for centuries, educated some of Ireland's brightest scholars.**

Higher Education

There are seven main centers of university-level programs in Ireland. The Republic's most prestigious educational institution is Trinity College in Dublin, a Protestant university to which Catholics were admitted only after 1970. Other institutions include University College, Dublin; Saint Patrick's College, Maynooth; Dublin City University; and the University of Limerick. The courses of study at these colleges are heavily influenced and funded by the government. Because higher education is largely paid for by the state, many Irish citizens can pursue college degrees without encountering pressing financial concerns.

A Predominantly Catholic Population

The majority of Irish people are Catholics. Christianity had already reached the island by the fifth century. In the twelfth century, Pope Adrian IV gave Britain's King Henry II a commission to reform the Irish Church. At that time, the British monarchy was still Catholic. When King Henry VIII established the Church of England as the official religion in the sixteenth century, the majority of the Irish remained faithful to Catholicism. British citizens who moved to Ireland brought Protestantism with them, settling mainly in Northern Ireland.

Today, an estimated 90 percent of residents in the Irish Republic are Catholic. In Northern Ireland, the majority of residents are Protestant. The clash between Protestants and Catholics there, over the question of Irish nationality, has posed problems for residents and visitors. While there are Protestants in the Republic of Ireland, too, no divide seems to exist between the different religious groups, mainly because there is no question of the Republic reverting to Protestant British rule.

In the Irish Republic, the Catholic Church runs most of the schools, as well as some hospitals and social services. The Church has also played an important role in politics, informing policies on issues such as divorce, contraception, abortion, and

SAINT PATRICK

Saint Patrick is Ireland's patron saint, and Saint Patrick's Day, on March 17, is celebrated with elaborate parades throughout Ireland.
(*A Closer Look, page 68*)

Left: These Catholic altar boys are part of a festival procession in County Cork.

homosexuality. In 1990, however, the election of Mary Robinson, a liberal lawyer, to the presidency introduced a political climate more favorable to women and generally seen, by men and women alike, as more enlightened on social and political issues.

Like most cosmopolitan European cities, Dublin, the capital of the Irish Republic, is home to a diversity of religious beliefs. In the rest of the country, however, there are only small pockets of minority religions outside of the Catholic and Protestant faiths. Minority religious groups include Jews and Muslims. Folk religions have dwindled over the past 1,500 years, and, today, most people simply enjoy the legends that remain, without taking them too seriously.

Language and Literature

Ireland was a Gaelic-speaking nation until the 1500s, when English increasingly became used for communication. Today, Gaelic and English are the official languages of Ireland. While about 11 percent of the population speaks Gaelic fluently, less than 2 percent uses it on a daily basis, at home or at work. As part of a drive to revive the language, all schoolchildren must now take classes in Gaelic. Proficiency in Gaelic is also required for entrance to universities and for careers in the public sector.

The Gaelic language has roots in Celtic, a subfamily of the Indo-European languages. The emphasis falls on the first syllable of almost every word. Accent marks and dots over certain letters indicate the lengths and sounds of the syllables. The Irish alphabet consists of eighteen letters — thirteen consonants and five vowels. Names in Ireland range from traditional Gaelic names to Christian names. Popular Gaelic names include *Sinead*

Above: **The Long Room library of Trinity College houses an astounding collection of books and manuscripts.**

THE BOOK OF KELLS

Housed in the Long Room library of Trinity College, Dublin, the ninth-century Book of Kells is one of the most important illuminated manuscripts in Ireland.

(A Closer Look, page 46)

(shin-NADE), *Liam* (LEE-am), *Sean* (SHAWN), and *Siobhan* (shi-VAWN). Traditional Irish Catholic names include *Patrick*, *Daniel*, *Colleen*, and *Mary*.

The Irish usage of English is similar to that of the British and other native English speakers, although the Irish pronounce English words slightly differently, and their sentences have a unique cadence.

The oral tradition of storytelling is a very important element of Irish culture and language. Stories are told either in verse, song, or prose. Some tales are based on folk legends, while others recount important family or historical events, such as the Great Famine. These stories are told at home, during festivals, in playhouses, or in public gathering places, such as pubs.

Ireland's storytelling tradition might well have contributed to its large output of famous writers, some of whom have moved to other countries, such as Britain or the United States. Well-known Irish authors include James Joyce and Frank McCourt, who recently wrote his memoirs entitled *Angela's Ashes: A Memoir of a Childhood*. Famous Irish playwrights include Samuel Beckett, Oscar Wilde, and George Bernard Shaw. William Butler Yeats and Seamus Heaney are among Ireland's finest poets.

Above: **A road sign in Ireland is posted in English and Gaelic.**

IRISH LITERARY GREATS

Poet W. B. Yeats *(below, left)* **and playwright George Bernard Shaw** *(below, right)* **rank among Ireland's acclaimed literary figures.**
(A Closer Look, page 58)

Arts

Music

While contemporary forms of music, such as rock and country and western, are popular in Ireland, it is traditional Irish music that captures the spirit of the country. Traditional music is played on a wide variety of instruments, including the button accordion, *uillean* (IL-lee-an) pipes (similar to bagpipes), harp, tin whistle, fiddle, and *bodhran* (BOAR-an), a type of drum. Bands are not restricted to a set group of instruments, and changing instruments and players between songs is common. Irish music is often accompanied by singing. Popular traditional songs range from medieval Gaelic love songs to nineteenth-century folk songs. Some well-loved traditional musicians are Liam O'Flionn, Paddy Keenan, and Christy Moore.

New musicians are constantly adapting traditional music to suit their talents and interests. Contemporary music has earned an increasing following, particularly since the rise of Irish bands, such as U2, on the world music scene. There has been a surge of interest in Irish music with musicians such as Enya, Sinead O'Connor, and the Chieftains, all of whom have fused old and new musical ideas to create a new tradition of Irish music.

THE IRISH MUSIC REVIVAL

Traditional Irish music made a comeback in the 1950s and 1960s through groups such as the Irish Music Movement. Today, Irish pop musicians, including U2, the Corrs, and Sinead O'Connor, are taking the world by storm.
(A Closer Look, page 60)

Left: Buskers, or street performers, entertain passersby on the streets of Killarney, in the southwestern part of the Irish Republic.

Left: **Young people are taking a renewed interest in traditional Irish dancing.**

Dancing

As a result of renewed interest in Irish culture, traditional Irish dancing, or step dancing, has become increasingly popular, in both urban and rural Ireland. In rural areas of the country, Sunday village dances have been the focus of social life since the 1600s. These dances, called *ceilis* (KAY-lees), combine traditional dancing and music. It was from these village dances that step dancing regained popularity.

Step dancing is a structured form that has groups of four single dancers or four pairs of dancers standing in a square. The dance is performed almost entirely with the legs and feet — the dancers' arms are usually held stiffly at their sides. Performers often wear elaborate traditional costumes with Gaelic designs and ballet-type shoes that are laced over the feet and ankles. Most step dancers are girls or women, although boys and men are becoming increasingly interested in the dance.

Architecture

Irish architecture encompasses many eras and changes and has suffered at the hands of its turbulent and often violent history. In the mid-1600s, Oliver Cromwell's forces destroyed many castles, monasteries, and towns in their efforts to quash Irish discontent. Surviving architectural sites include prehistoric passage tombs, Iron Age ring forts, stone round towers, tower houses, and castles. Irish homes range from simple thatched-roof cottages to palatial mansions built by prosperous landlords in the nineteenth century. Many of Ireland's most impressive architectural sites are open to the public.

Above: **Dromoland Castle in County Galway is open to the public.**

Below: **This entrance in Merrion Square, Dublin, is an early twentieth-century Georgian doorway.**

Traditional Crafts

The tourist trade has been largely responsible for reviving interest in traditional Irish crafts, although some were thriving even before Ireland became a major tourist destination. Textiles are among the most traditional of the Irish crafts. They include woolen sweaters and woven wool clothing, products made from Irish linen, such as bedclothes and tablecloths, and handmade Irish lace. Jewelry-making is another traditional craft. Today, jewelers often base their designs on traditional Celtic patterns and myths or on local plants and wildlife. Perhaps the most

common piece of Irish jewelry is the Claddagh ring, which is a traditional Irish betrothal ring. Other popular ornaments are enameled brooches and pendants. Small sculptures and reliefs are carved out of the peat found in Ireland. These carvings are inspired by creatures, both real and mythical, that also appear in other Gaelic arts and crafts or in early Christian artwork. Other craftspeople make pottery, musical instruments, or fine glassware, such as Waterford or Tyrone crystal.

On Location in Ireland

Ireland has become a popular location for films, a trend that began in the early 1950s when American movie legend John Wayne starred in *The Quiet Man*, which was filmed in an Irish village called Cong. Since then, Ireland has provided the backdrop for films ranging from Irish legends (*Into the West* and *The Secret of Roan Inish*) to Irish politics (*In the Name of the Father* and *Some Mother's Son*).

Some of the films that have been made about Ireland have been based on books written by Irish writers, such as Roddy Doyle's *The Commitments*. Other films are based on Irish people, such as Josef Locke, a famous Irish tenor who is the subject of the movie *Hear My Song*, and Michael Collins, a famous revolutionary leader of the IRA, who is the subject of a movie that bears his name.

CELTIC HISTORY AND ART

The earliest Celtic relics date back to the Bronze and Iron Ages, more than three thousand years ago. Later Celtic art shows Greek and Roman influences.
(A Closer Look, page 52)

THE NEWGRANGE PASSAGE TOMB

One of the most spectacular examples of prehistoric architecture, the Newgrange Passage Tomb is believed to be the burial chamber of an important person.
(A Closer Look, page 64)

Left: **Irish actor Liam Neeson plays the title role in *Michael Collins*, a film about one of Ireland's most important patriots.**

Leisure and Festivals

Leisure Activities

The Irish are sociable people who enjoy getting together with family and friends. Some of the favorite activities in Ireland include gardening, singing, taking care of pets, and playing or listening to music. The Irish also like getting out and enjoying nature by walking, going boating or fishing, or participating in other outdoor activities, such as Gaelic football.

Songs and Stories

Music and storytelling have a cherished place in Irish culture. Traditional music, involving instruments and singers, evolved at a time when there were no radios or television sets. People depended on traveling bards, or wandering singers who composed songs, for news of what was going on elsewhere on their island home. The tradition never died, and music is an important part of Irish life today. Anyone present at a pub can participate in the music and singing. Stories can be either set to

Below: **Residents of Lismore, in County Waterford, enjoy a leisurely afternoon.**

music or told straight. Legends and contemporary stories are equally popular. Most important are the skill and wit of the storyteller — and the Irish excel at this art.

The Irish Pub

Pubs are among the best places to spend a relaxing evening out in Ireland. These social centers are combination bars and restaurants, where people can have meals and enjoy the company of friends, colleagues, neighbors, or families. Children often accompany their parents to pubs, eating and interacting with the adults, although they are not allowed to drink alcohol.

GAA Clubs

The Gaelic Athletic Association (GAA) was founded in 1884 to promote traditional Irish sports and discourage British influence. Funded by the state, the association has a membership of over 800,000 and has been described as the most powerful organization in the Republic, second only to the Catholic Church.

GAA clubs, consisting of sports as well as social centers, are open only to Irish members and their guests. The social clubs have bars and restaurants. GAA members pay low annual dues to enjoy club facilities.

IRISH MYTHS AND LEGENDS

The Irish tradition of storytelling comes from Ireland's Celtic past, when professional storytellers, called druids, spun tales of revenge and heroism.
(A Closer Look, page 62)

Sports

Two of the most popular traditional games in the Irish Republic are Gaelic football, which is still a favorite sport in Ireland, and hurling, a fast, field sport played with sticks that resemble those used in hockey. Gaelic football is similar to soccer and rugby in that it is played with a ball on a field. Girls and women play a game similar to hurling, called camogie. These sports are played entirely at the amateur level. Other popular sports in Ireland are soccer, rugby, golf, darts, horse racing, and fishing. Except for darts and fishing, all of these are professional sports. Horse racing, soccer, and rugby are also international sports.

Most people in Ireland are either zealous participants or enthusiastic spectators in sporting events. Gaelic football fever breaks out all over the Republic of Ireland when teams compete in the All-Ireland finals in Dublin. Soccer is a close second to Gaelic football as the favorite sport of the country. World Cup games are closely followed, especially after the Irish team made it to the quarter-finals in the 1990 World Cup and the final runoffs in 1994.

Golf is enjoyed by men and women alike. More than three hundred golf courses dot the island. Over fifty of them are championship class courses, which host international competitions and attract professional golfers from around the world. Because Ireland is surrounded by the ocean, many of the courses have spectacular views of the Irish coast.

Horse racing is not an elitist sport in Ireland; it attracts a wide base of fans. Some of the biggest horse racing events are the Irish Grand National, a steeplechase run in County Meath; the Irish Derby, the premier flat race that draws many of Europe's best horses and horse owners; and the Dublin Horse Show, Ireland's most famous horse show, with racing and jumping events.

Cycling and Sean Kelly

Cycling has a somewhat smaller following than some of the other sports. Nevertheless, it provided Ireland with one of its most famous sports figures, Sean Kelly, who won the prestigious Tour de France in 1988. Kelly grew up on a farm in southern Ireland and learned to cycle on Ireland's small country roads, eventually rising through the ranks of international cycling in Europe. His talent earned him the nickname "King of the Road." The president of Ireland presented him with an award for his role as an unofficial ambassador for Ireland and for his services to his sport. In 1989, Kelly was named European of the Year, and, in an unusual move, his home town named a square after him, an honor usually reserved for great people who have died.

Left: **The Irish Derby is attended by people from all walks of life.**

Major Festivals

Ireland celebrates festivals throughout the year, although most of these celebrations take place in the warmer spring, summer, and autumn seasons.

Religious festivals center primarily around Saint Patrick's Day, the Blessing of the Sea, and Saint Stephen's Day. Of these, Saint Patrick's Day (March 17) is, by far, the most widely celebrated. Its festivities include parades, musical events, and pilgrimages throughout Ireland, particularly in the cities of Dublin, Downpatrick, Cork, Limerick, and Armagh. Saint Patrick's Day celebrates the famous saint who, legend has it,

Below: **A bagpipe band plays rousing traditional music on Saint Patrick's Day.**

drove all the snakes from Ireland. In fact, Saint Patrick was an early Christian missionary to the island — though not the first — who lived and worked in the fifth century.

Many secular festivals, such as the Adare Jazz Festival, the Cork Jazz Festival, Feis Ceoil, the Pan Celtic Festival, and the Ballyshannon International Folk Festival, focus on music. Some, such as the Galway Arts Festival, the Letterkenny Folk Festival, and the Puck Fair, center around the arts and traditional culture. Still others focus on specific events or objects, such as the Galway Oyster Festival and Shamhana (Halloween). Sporting events, such as the Cork Regatta Week, often become festive occasions, too.

The Kilkenny Arts Week, held annually in the fourth week of August, is arguably Ireland's top arts festival. It features the work of local craftspeople and artists, highlighting poetry, films, crafts, and classical music.

The Lisdoonvarna Matchmaking Festival is another popular event. It takes place in the town of Lisdoonvarna, on Ireland's west coast. Originally, the celebration was a harvesttime event, in which couples were matched because there were few opportunities for villagers to travel and meet other people. Today, the Lisdoonvarna Matchmaking Festival is a fun and festive occasion that takes place during the entire month of

Below: **Irish girls perform in a Children's Day parade.**

September and the first week of October, a period that still coincides with the annual harvest. People gather in dance halls and pubs to sing, dance, and listen to music. They also keep an eye open for potential partners.

Public Holidays

Ireland's public holidays include New Year's Day, Saint Patrick's Day, Good Friday, Easter Monday, May Day, June Bank Holiday, August Bank Holiday, October Bank Holiday, Christmas, and Saint Stephen's Day. Bank holidays are days on which all banks and many businesses are closed.

Food

Left: Roast lamb is a favorite dish in Ireland.

Traditionally, Irish people started the day with very large breakfasts, consisting of fried eggs, bacon or sausages, grilled tomatoes, brown bread, and black or white pudding (a type of meat sausage). This big breakfast is called a "fry." Dinner, served at midday, was the main meal, and a lighter meal, called "tea," was served later in the day. This meal pattern was established to facilitate the hardworking lifestyles of farmers and day laborers. As lifestyles changed, however, so did the eating habits of people in more modern jobs. Today, many Irish people eat a lighter breakfast and midday meal, then enjoy a larger meal at the end of the working day, when they are home with their families. The traditional Irish fry, however, can still be found in hotels and bed and breakfast inns, and pubs still serve huge midday meals.

Irish Fare

Popular Irish food includes lamb, Irish stew, homemade cheeses, fresh fish of many varieties, and freshly baked breads and scones

Below: Irish coffee is a delicious concoction of coffee, Irish whiskey, and cream.

(a light bread). Fish and chips, a meal of fish fried in batter and served with french fried potatoes, is sold in shops that are affectionately called "chippers." The Irish enjoy a wide variety of vegetables, including potatoes, cabbages, carrots, and mushrooms.

Eating in Ireland

The Irish are very family oriented, and meals, eaten with family members, are an important part of daily life. Utensils, cooking techniques, and dining etiquette in Ireland, both at home and at social functions, is much the same as in other Western countries.

Pubs serve bar snacks that include hearty soups, toasted sandwiches (typically a combination of ham, cheese, and onions), and chips. The Irish love their rich, dark beer and Irish coffee, which is a mixture of coffee, cream, and whiskey. A wide assortment of soft drinks is on the menu, too. Family-style restaurants offer wholesome, plain cooking at affordable prices. In the past, foreign cuisines were rare in Ireland, but, today, cities such as Dublin boast French, Italian, and Russian restaurants.

Below: **This couple is dining at a unique medieval banquet.**

A CLOSER LOOK AT IRELAND

There is a popular saying that good things come in small packages, and Ireland is no exception. Its place in history is well established, and the country has many exciting aspects. This section offers a glimpse into some fascinating features of Irish culture, ranging from ancient Celtic relics and structures, such as the Newgrange Passage Tomb, to environmental issues, such as the depletion of peat, a precious natural resource. Learn about the myths and legends of this land, as well as about the recent troubled past of the Irish people. Discover, too, the longstanding Irish literary and musical traditions that have produced world-class cultural figures, from James Joyce and William Butler Yeats to Sinead O'Connor and U2.

Opposite: Two Irish girls sit astride a sculpture of two women with shopping bags, affectionately called *Hags with Bags*, at Ormond Quay in Dublin city.

Below: The facade of the Chancery Inn in Dublin is eye-catching. Pubs like this one are the Irish people's favorite social meeting places, where they exchange news and play traditional music.

The Aran Islands

The Aran Islands are located off the western coast of Ireland, close to the mouth of Galway Bay. The largest island is Inishmore, followed by Inishmaan and Inisheer. These islands were formed thousands of years ago from a limestone ridge. Famed for their beautiful coastal views, the Aran Islands are crisscrossed with stone walls. Christianity was introduced to the islands many centuries ago, and ancient monasteries dot the landscape. Today, the Aran Islands are largely protected from mainstream influences and have maintained a strong traditional Irish culture. Most Aran Islanders work as farmers or fishermen, or are in the tourist trade.

Ancient Stone Forts

Many large prehistoric stone forts remain on the Aran Islands, chiefly on Inishmore. This island's notable forts include Dun Eoghanachta, Dun Eochla, Dun Aonghasa, and Dun Duchathair. Dating back to the Iron or Bronze Age, more than three thousand years ago, Dun Aonghasa and Dun Duchathair are promontory forts, or semicircular structures built into the edges of cliff walls. The inhabitants of these forts were protected from invasions by

Left: **Charming thatch-roofed cottages sit alongside more modern houses on Inisheer, the smallest of the Aran Islands.**

Above: **Hand-knitted Aran sweaters are very popular in Ireland.**

steep, high cliffs. Dun Aonghasa has four concentric stone walls and is also encircled by a ring of razor-sharp pointed stone stakes. Dun Duchathair is known for its dry-stone ramparts. Dun Eoghanachta and Dun Eochla are inland forts built slightly later than the other two.

The Aran Lifestyle

The lifestyle and culture of the people on the Aran Islands are very different from those on the Irish mainland. There are few cars on the island roads; most people cycle or ride in jaunting cars, a kind of horse-drawn carriage. Many islanders still wear traditional Aran dress, which consists of red flannel skirts and crocheted shawls for women, and sleeveless tweed jackets and colorful knitted belts for men.

The Aran Islanders are famous for their beautiful knitwear. Aran wool sweaters have detailed knitting stitches and are usually oiled to make the garment resistant to wet weather. According to tradition, each Aran family had a distinctive sweater pattern. This pattern helped them identify relatives drowned at sea, whose bodies had otherwise become unrecognizable.

The Book of Kells

Illuminated manuscripts are texts illustrated with elaborate and colorful drawings. These ancient manuscripts contained religious writings and were prepared primarily by monks. Ireland boasts a number of illuminated manuscripts, the most beautiful and valuable of which is the Book of Kells.

The Four Gospels

No one knows for certain who created the Book of Kells, but this work is often attributed to ninth-century Christian monks from the island of Iona, who fled that island after it was raided by Vikings. The Book of Kells contains a Latin translation of the Four Gospels, written in beautiful calligraphy (an elegant form of script done with pen and ink). Several copies of the book were made to protect it from destruction. The original was moved to Trinity College in the seventeenth century. Today, two volumes of the book are displayed in climate-controlled glass cases in the university's Long Room library. A page of the book is turned every day, so viewers may read and admire different pages. This procedure also prevents the pages from degenerating due to overexposure to light.

Creating the Book of Kells

The calligraphy in the Book of Kells is embellished with interlacing spirals and animal and human figures, many of which symbolize Christian lessons and ideas. Some of the pages are mainly composed of text, while others are entirely pictorial. The scribes who copied the text often enlarged the first letters of sentences and decorated them with beautiful painted patterns. At the ends of sentences, the scribes often painted animal or human forms. Decorated capitals, or monograms, consisting of two or more letters combined into an intricate design, fill some pages. Other pages depict biblical scenes.

Most of the dyes used to create the colors in the book were locally made, but some of the rarer colors were imported from as far as the Middle East. The painstaking effort put into obtaining these costly materials reflects the great importance of these documents to their medieval makers.

Above: **The text in the Book of Kells is written in beautiful, rounded calligraphy, with the first letters of each sentence artfully decorated.**

Opposite: **A page from the wonderfully crafted Book of Kells shows the Virgin Mary and the infant Jesus.**

47

The Burren

The Burren is a vast limestone plateau in the western part of Ireland, in County Clare. It encompasses approximately 193 square miles (500 square km) of land. The name *Burren* comes from the Gaelic word *boireann* (BWIR-ren), which means "rocky land" or "the rock." The northern section of the Burren includes mountains that rise majestically above the surrounding landscape, while the southern section runs into the Cliffs of Moher, which are made of black shale and sandstone.

Life in the Burren

The Burren has a unique microclimate that allows plants from both tropical and alpine areas to thrive. It is made of limestone, a soft, porous rock. Wind, water, and glacial ice, which crossed over Ireland during the Ice Ages several thousand years ago, eroded deep crevices, or grykes, in the Burren's limestone. An extensive cave system carved out by running water is concealed

Below: **The Poulnabrone Dolmen in the Burren is a portal tomb that dates back to approximately 3300 B.C., during the Neolithic period.**

Above: **Limestone slabs are scattered throughout the Burren.**

beneath the surface of the plateau. These underground reservoirs, or turloughs, are the most unusual features of the area, and they support many plants and animals. Vents from the Burren's underground caves supply heat to Mediterranean plant species during the winter and cool air and water to the alpine plants during the summer. Some of the more common plants found in the Burren include the mountain avens (an alpine species), the maidenhair fern (a Mediterranean plant), the hoary rock rose, the holly tree, the juniper, the gnarled blackthorn, and the bloody cranesbill. Many varieties of orchids also grow in the Burren, including the bee orchid and the lesser butterfly orchid. All these plants grow in the rock crevices, where they are afforded protection from strong winds and from grazing cattle.

Besides cows, sheep, and goats, the Burren hosts Irish hares, Whooper swans, hooded crows, skylarks, and cuckoos in the mountains, as well as razorbills and puffins on the coast. The Burren is also home to twenty-eight species of butterflies.

Below: **The bloody cranesbill adds a dash of color to the barren landscape of the Burren.**

Castles in Ireland

The Irish landscape is sprinkled with stone castles, some almost a thousand years old, built by Irish chiefs to defend their territories from rival chiefs or from English settlers. Many of these castles are simple, two-story, circular or square structures, with narrow windows and staircases. Larger, multi-room castles, however, consist of several buildings grouped closely together and surrounded by outer walls for protection.

As a further deterrent to unwelcome visitors, castles were usually located on manmade islands in lakes or on hilltops that provided commanding views of the surrounding countryside. Many also had defensive features, such as outer wall enclosures; machicolations (projecting parapets); and crenelated walls (stone walls with evenly spaced slits), which allowed soldiers to attack enemies from protected positions.

Below: **Dublin's Malahide Castle lies northeast of the city center and is a popular tourist attraction.**

Ireland's Castles Today

In the 1600s, Sir Oliver Cromwell's British forces, charged with putting down Catholic rebellions against unfair land policies, destroyed many castles throughout Ireland. Cromwell's policy was to raze any stronghold that might threaten the power of the British king or his followers in Ireland. By the time Cromwell's forces reached the western coast of Ireland, however, they felt that the castles in this part of the island were too far away to represent any kind of real threat. As a result, many castles in western Ireland are still standing, particularly in County Clare, although several are in a state of disrepair and neglect.

Some of these castles have been restored to their original condition, while others have been renovated to have modern conveniences, such as electricity and running water. Larger castles that have been restored often host tours and banquets or serve as historical museums. Bunratty Castle in County Limerick is a popular venue for celebrations. Some of the smaller castles have been restored privately and are used as homes or vacation rental units.

Above: Today, many of Ireland's castles, such as the Rock of Cashel in southern Ireland, are open for visitors to investigate, unsupervised. Regardless of their condition and their current uses, the castles are powerful reminders of Ireland's history.

Celtic History and Art

The Celts came to Ireland from Central Europe by way of France and Britain. Celtic influence spread quickly throughout Europe but their traditions survived more intact in Ireland than in other European countries because many of these countries were subjected to further invasion by the Romans, who never reached the shores of Ireland.

Celtic societies were made up of people with a common cultural heritage rather than shared physical traits. These societies were hierarchical, and the powers of the chiefs of each tribe took on kinglike qualities. The Celts were pagans and relied on druids, or learned men, for spiritual guidance. In the fifth century, Christianity slowly won over the Celts in Ireland. By the end of the eighth century, Celtic tribal life in Ireland had been effectively destroyed by Viking invaders to the island. The legacy of the Celts, however, was retained through legends, myths, and art. The Celtic civilization continues to influence Ireland's character today.

Celtic Art

Celtic art was influenced by Greek and Roman culture. One of the earliest surviving pieces of Celtic artistry is the ritual Turoe stone,

Left: **Celtic society had a rigid class structure, in which groups of people served a king or chieftain.**

Left: Celtic High Crosses were carved with traditional Celtic designs or with scenes from the Old and New Testaments. These crosses were probably used as illustrated Bibles, to instruct the common people.

a large boulder with spirals, stylized plant forms, and curves carved across its surface. The stone dates back to the second or third century B.C. Celtic designs were also used to decorate bronze objects, such as spear butts, scabbards, and iron spear heads.

The advent of Christianity was accompanied by a wave of creative crafts. The ornate designs of the early Celts were stylized and used as decorations on jewelry, plaques, armor, and in illuminated manuscripts. Religious objects, such as chalices, bells, and shrines, rank among the most beautiful examples of Celtic art. Later craftsmen added color through enameling and by using colored glass and semiprecious stones. Perhaps the most recognized Christian-era Celtic objects are the High Crosses, tall stone crosses with circles that overlie the arms of the crosses.

The Great Famine

In the nineteenth century, potatoes were an essential part of the diet of the Irish peasant class, and there was no widely available substitute. From 1845 to 1848, a blight hit Ireland's potato farms; the potatoes simply rotted in the ground, yielding an inedible crop. The potato blight resulted in mass starvation and, particularly among the Irish peasant classes, large-scale emigration. By 1852, at least one million people had died of disease or starvation, and an additional one million had emigrated from Ireland. In total, the country lost 25 percent of its population in a period of just six years. The potato famine continued to plague the Irish, and by 1901, an additional two million people had died or left the country. The population, then, was half of what it had been prior to 1845. In many parts of Ireland, entire towns and communities were wiped out by the famine.

The Great Famine fell at a time when antiunion forces, who wanted to disband the legal union between Britain and Ireland, were gathering support. The famine put those efforts on hold, while the plight of the Irish peasantry became a focus for

Left: **Many Irish were evicted from their homes by their British landlords during the Great Famine, when the Irish could no longer afford to pay the rent.**

Above: **In the mid-nineteenth century, Irish families crowded the harbors with all their possessions, in the hope for a new life in the United States.**

nationalist groups. During the famine, Irish grain crops that could have fed starving Irish people were being exported to Great Britain, fueling anti-British sentiment in Ireland.

A New Life Overseas

Many of the émigrés, or emigrants, who fled Ireland at this time moved to the United States. Others fled to Australia, Britain, and other European countries. By the hundreds, they boarded ships bound for America. Unfortunately, many of these ships were overcrowded and rife with sickness, and many people died before the so-called "coffin ships" reached their destination. The survivors paved the way for a large Irish community in the United States. Although most of the Irish immigrants entering the United States were from rural parts of Ireland, they settled largely in bustling New York City, close to where the ships landed at Castle Garden. The mass migrations established a strong connection between the United States and Ireland — one that continues today.

The History of "the Troubles"

"The Troubles" refers to the clash between Protestant and Catholic militant groups in Northern Ireland. The main Catholic militant force, the Irish Republican Army (IRA), wants to unite Northern Ireland and the Republic of Ireland, and thereby cut all ties between Great Britain and Northern Ireland. The Protestant groups, on the other hand, want to maintain ties with Britain.

The Troubles has roots in the sixteenth century, when the British controlled all of Ireland and imposed Protestantism as the dominant religion. Irish Catholics rebelled against the system, and the English monarchy responded by implementing the Penal Laws, which deprived Catholics of all land rights. Protestants from Great Britain soon colonized large areas of the northern parts of Ireland, where Catholics had been removed from their land, thus creating a large Protestant stronghold.

In 1914, home rule was enacted, enabling the Irish to govern their own country, with the provision that Northern Ireland should remain part of Great Britain for an additional six years. Home rule was suspended, however, for the duration of World War I and was never revived. In 1921, negotiations to alleviate

Left: **Riots have plagued Northern Ireland in the last few decades. Many lives have been lost and much property has been damaged.**

Left: **Thousands of Irish march to commemorate the twenty-sixth anniversary of Bloody Sunday in Londonderry.**

some of the civil unrest led to the partition of Ireland. The northern, Protestant region would remain tied to Britain. The southern, Catholic region became known as the Irish Free State. This agreement, however, failed to appease factions that wanted either complete union with Britain or complete independence, and civil war broke out.

In 1949, the Irish Free State declared its independence from England. In the late 1950s and early 1960s, the IRA began using terrorist tactics along the border between the two countries, beginning a long campaign to win Northern Ireland's freedom from Britain. In 1972, British soldiers killed thirteen Irish demonstrators in Londonderry in an incident now known as Bloody Sunday. After this incident, the terrorist tactics of the IRA and Protestant groups increased. Peace talks were initiated many times, but no agreement lasted.

In the spring of 1998, Protestants and Catholics began another round of discussions aimed at ending the Troubles. For the first time, Sinn Fein, the political wing of the IRA, was allowed to join in the talks. On Good Friday, 1998, a peace agreement was reached and was overwhelmingly approved by vote, both in Northern Ireland and in the Republic of Ireland. The Republic agreed to retract its historical claims to Northern Ireland, which gained more autonomy from Britain. The implications of this agreement for the future of Ireland are uncertain, particularly as Protestant groups have mounted violent protests, but the Irish are optimistic that the Good Friday Agreement could be a first step toward peace on the island.

Irish Literary Greats

Irish literature — creative, lyrical, insightful, provocative — ranges from rural to urban experiences, across the Gaelic and English languages, and over centuries of time. Nobel Prize winners George Bernard Shaw, William Butler Yeats, and Samuel Beckett all came from this impressive literary tradition.

Early Literature

Celtic sagas, first recorded some five hundred years ago, are the oldest form of Irish literature. These epics told of war, culture, and romance in ancient times. This literary form faded in importance in the seventeenth century, when the Irish aristocracy for whom it was written fell apart. Gaelic literature has, however, experienced several revivals since then and is still written today.

The Anglo-Irish

Ireland has not always been viewed as an open-minded country conducive to writing. From the eighteenth century onward, many Irish writers moved to England and made it their new home.

Left: **The Abbey Theatre, Dublin, is shown here as it looked in the early twentieth century. It was entirely rebuilt some thirty or more years ago. The Theatre has helped revive literary and dramatic traditions in Ireland.**

They were called Anglo-Irish writers, a group that included Jonathan Swift, author of *Gulliver's Travels* and numerous political pamphlets and satires; Oscar Wilde, who wrote *The Importance of Being Earnest* and other works of drama and fiction; and George Bernard Shaw, whose play *Pygmalion* was to influence succeeding generations of playwrights. Although these authors left Ireland, they took part of their home country with them, and Irish themes often recurred in their work.

Above, left: **Celebrated poet Seamus Heaney won the Whitbread Book of the Year award in 1996 for his work *The Spirit Level.***

Above, right: **James Joyce's works include *Dubliners, Ulysses,* and *Finnegan's Wake.* Joyce captured the flavor of Dublin and rural Ireland in his experimental style of writing. His innovative use of language and narrative techniques greatly influenced the development of the modern novel.**

Literature Today

In the twentieth century, Ireland became a more fashionable home for writers, due in part to the founding of the Abbey Theatre in Dublin by Yeats and Lady Gregory in 1898. The opening of the Abbey in 1904 heralded the Irish Revival, a movement that helped forge a new national and cultural identity by bringing Irish national and local themes to the forefront of literature and drama. Many important playwrights had their works performed at the Abbey Theatre.

Today, Ireland continues to produce prominent authors, among whom are William Trevor, Brian Moore, Roddy Doyle, Brian Friel, and Edna O'Brien. Ireland's contemporary poets, Seamus Heaney and Derek Mahon of Northern Ireland, are considered among the most outstanding in the world.

The Irish Music Revival

Traditional Irish music has been described as having a reflective, spiritual quality that reaches back into the ancient past. Some attribute its soulfulness to a history of persecution. Under British rule, Irish culture was suppressed, and Irish music was outlawed for a time. For the people who sang and played it, therefore, it became associated with the plight of the Irish themselves and with nationalist pride. Driven underground, Irish music remained pure in form, relatively unmixed with other musical forms. It resurfaced in the twentieth century, and, in the 1950s, a great deal of concern was voiced that the music of Ireland was being lost in an influx of foreign music. This issue was confronted in the 1950s and 1960s by groups set on reviving traditional Irish music. One of them was the Comhaltas Ceoltoiri Eireann (CCE), or the Irish Music Movement.

Above: One of the best places to listen to traditional Irish music is at an Irish pub.

The Irish Music Movement organized festivals and music classes in the 1950s. By the 1960s, there was a tremendous increase in Irish music groups. The Chieftains, a group still popular today, had their beginnings in the Irish Music Movement. Another influence on the traditional Irish music scene came from musicians of Irish descent who were performing and recording music abroad, particularly in the United States. When Irish music underwent a revival in Ireland, some of these musicians moved back to Ireland to be part of the movement.

Renewed interest in traditional Irish music led to the rise of a new form — Irish rock. Some of the earlier Irish rock acts include Horslips, Van Morrison, and the Pogues. These musicians drew heavily on the Irish musical tradition. Irish rock has now spread throughout the world through successful musicians such as Sinead O'Connor and groups such as U2. While their music is not directly derived from traditional Irish music, the content and expression of their sentiments is clearly in the Irish tradition. U2's music, in particular, includes political and social commentary — one of its songs is entitled *Sunday Bloody Sunday*. The popularity of Irish music in other countries has led to an increased sense of musical and cultural self-confidence in Irish musicians.

Left: **Bono fronts one of Ireland's most popular rock groups, U2, whose early songs reflected the frustrations, anger, and political aspirations of the Irish people.**

Irish Myths and Legends

Ireland's rich tradition of myths and legends began centuries ago, when the Celts ruled the island. These stories range from tales of everyday events to epic sagas along the lines of famous Greek and Roman tales. Historically, these tales were told primarily by druids, a group of professional learned men, whose training required them to memorize and recite as many as 350 stories of Irish kings, gods, and goddesses.

Scholars have classified these legends into four primary categories: the Mythological Cycle, with stories of the Celtic gods and goddesses and their exploits; the Historical Cycle, with stories of various Irish kings; the Ulster Cycle, with stories of the warriors of Ulster, in northern Ireland, including tales of the young hero Cuchulainn; and the Fenian Cycle, with stories that revolve around Finn MacCool, a legendary Irish hero.

The protagonists of Irish tales were usually giants and skilled warriors, the most famous of which is Cuchulainn, who would swell to a giant's size and turn different colors before a battle. Another famous warrior, Finn MacCool, possessed great battle skill as well as the amazing supernatural powers of a seer.

Left: Druids told of ancient Celtic gods and goddesses in the Mythological Cycle. These learned men also taught that the soul did not die but passed on to another body after the one it inhabited died. The Otherworld, said to be on an island off the western coast of Ireland, features prominently in these stories. Today, Ireland has societies that reenact ancient Celtic rituals.

Left: **One of the most frightening spirits in Irish folklore is the banshee. People believed that this female spirit wailed outside a house to signal the death of someone within.**

Fairies and leprechauns, or the "little people," play major roles in Irish folktales. Fairies were said to dwell in mounds of earth, or fairy raths, and it was commonly believed that touching one of these brought bad luck. Even today, many Irish farmers leave mounds in their fields untouched. Leprechauns, on the other hand, were said to bring good luck if you could catch them, because they would lead you to a pot of gold. If you took your eyes off them, however, they would disappear in an instant.

Myths and legends are so firmly planted in Irish memory and so strongly associated with the landscape that no matter where a person goes in Ireland, he or she is sure to encounter a place with legendary significance — a mound where Queen Maeve is said to be buried; or an undisturbed patch of land in the center of a field, where fairies are thought to dwell; or a mysterious lake, where Finn MacCool killed a dragon.

The Newgrange Passage Tomb

Passage tombs were ancient circular structures built to honor important people after they died. Underground passages led straight back to the center of the mound, where a burial chamber was built.

Ireland's most famous passage tomb is at Newgrange, in County Meath. The Newgrange Passage Tomb was built around 3200 B.C. Remarkably, it was not destroyed by any of Ireland's invaders, although grave robbers looted it. In the 1960s, archaeologists excavating Newgrange discovered that, during the Winter Solstice (December 21) every year, the sun's rays enter the tomb's entrance, travel along the 62-foot (19-m) passage, and light up the very center of the burial chamber. This phenomenon makes Newgrange the oldest known solar observatory in the world.

According to archaeologists, the original Newgrange structure took approximately seventy years to complete. The tomb is almost 200 feet (61 m) across, from one side of the mound to the other. It was built by people who did not have the use of

Below: The ancient Newgrange Passage Tomb took more than seventy years to complete. Modern restoration work was done between 1962 and 1975 to preserve this ancient site.

Left: Newgrange is an architectural wonder. On December 21, every year, sunlight enters the roof box above the entrance and illuminates the very center of the burial chamber.

the wheel or of metal tools. Nevertheless, they were able to transport about 200,000 tons (181,500 metric tons) of loose stones to build the mound that protects the burial chamber. They also transported huge slabs to make a circle around the outside of the mound. These slabs, many decorated with spiral, zigzag, and other geometric carvings, are about 4 feet (1.2 m) high and about 10 feet (3 m) long. Additional standing slabs line the passage and the burial chamber and mark the entrance. Horizontal slabs provide a roof for the entire passage and burial chamber.

The burial chamber itself is round, with three recessed side chambers. The dome-shaped ceiling reaches a height of 20 feet (6 m) above the floor. Inside the burial chamber are several basin-shaped chiseled stones, which would have contained funerary offerings and the bones of the dead.

Peatland

Peatland, or bog, a nonrenewable natural resource, is found in Europe, North America, and northern Asia. It covers about 15 percent of Ireland's landscape and exists in two main forms: blanket bog and raised bog. Blanket bog is found primarily in western Ireland, in mountainous areas, and in wetlands. Raised bogs are more often found in the middle of the island. Rich in partially decomposed, organic material that has been compressed over thousands of years, peat is used extensively for fuel, as well

Below: **Peat cutters harvest peat with shovels, special machinery, and other implements.**

as for fertilizer. Because peat is being harvested more quickly than it can regenerate, areas of peatland are rapidly vanishing.

From Lake Vegetation to Organic Fuel

Peat bogs developed over a long period of time. They began as shallow lakes left after the Ice Ages thousands of years ago. These lakes gradually filled with mud, where marsh or fen plants grew. Over the next several thousand years, vegetation continually grew and died and sank to the bottom of the muddy lake, where it formed the first layer of peat. This layer and subsequent layers did not decompose completely because of the lack of oxygen in the muddy water. Instead, the peat layers slowly spread out and built up. After about three thousand more years of this continual accumulation process, the lakes were filled with peat.

Today, peat is harvested by peat cutters who dig into the bogs, using shovel-like tools, called slanes, or using peat-harvesting machinery. They extract large blocks of peat, which are cut into smaller bricks and dried. The peat is then sold as fuel, called turf, to burn in fireplaces in homes.

The majority of people in Ireland still use peat bricks to heat their homes. Because of the dampness and the rainy climate, fires are built year-round in some places.

Below: **These young peat harvesters are loading peat into the back of a wagon.**

Large-scale peat harvesting has greatly diminished the extent of bog areas in Ireland. Peat burns readily, producing considerable quantities of smoke and ash. Because peat burning causes air pollution in densely populated areas, the city of Dublin outlawed the burning of this fuel. Peat harvesting also threatens the survival of the unique plants and animals supported by the unusual peatland habitat. The distinctive flora and fauna of the bogs include sphagnum mosses, bog cotton, bog asphodel, and a variety of dragonflies. Aside, however, from the occasional ban on burning peat, no other measures have been carried out to protect peatland from destruction.

Saint Patrick

Saint Patrick arrived on Ireland's shores as a missionary in 432 A.D. Although he is often credited with bringing Christianity to Ireland, it is almost certain that other missionaries had preceded him and laid the groundwork for establishing Christianity on the island.

The son of a Roman official who lived in western Britain, Saint Patrick was kidnapped by Irish raiders and taken to Ireland at the age of sixteen. There, he tended sheep for six years, before escaping back to Britain. He then trained abroad to be a cleric, probably in Gaul (now France). Returning to Britain, he had a

Left: **In the fifth century, Saint Patrick traveled through Ireland, preaching the Gospel and building churches.**

dream in which the Irish people were crying for him to return to their island. So Saint Patrick spent the following thirty years traveling through Ireland, converting Irish people to Christianity and establishing churches. He chose Armagh, in Northern Ireland, as the religious capital of Ireland.

Saint Patrick encountered some opposition in his early ministry, but stories are told of how he surmounted it. On Easter Sunday, A.D. 433, he lit a fire on the Hill of Slane to symbolize the arrival of Christianity in Ireland. This act was in defiance of an order from the High King of Tara, but when Patrick explained himself, the king was apparently impressed and granted him permission to preach the Gospel to the people there. Saint Patrick found novel ways to explain his faith to nonbelievers. According to one story, he used a shamrock, a three-leaved clover with a single stem, to describe the Christian concept of the Holy Trinity as three separate Persons united in one God.

In A.D. 441, Saint Patrick spent the forty days of Lent on Croagh Patrick, a mountain sacred to the pagan god Crom, and claimed the site for Christianity. Legend has it that when Saint Patrick rang his iron bell — said to have been blackened from hell's fires when he battled against the gods on Croagh Patrick — all the toads and snakes, except for one (the natterjack toad) leaped from the mountain to their deaths. Saint Patrick is, therefore, credited with ridding Ireland of all but one reptile forever. The ringing of his bell was also said to have released the children of the ocean god, Lir, from a spell that had turned them into swans to swim in the waters of a lake for 300 years.

Above: **The statue of Saint Patrick on Croagh Patrick is visited by thousands of Irish pilgrims every year.**

In Honor of Saint Patrick

Today, tens of thousands of pilgrims make their way to Croagh Patrick in pilgrimages that take place throughout the year. The main pilgrimage is held on the Sunday before the Lughnasa feast on August 1. On this day, more than 60,000 people make the two-hour ascent from the abbey at the mountain's base to the summit, where mass is celebrated.

Saint Patrick's Day, March 17, is celebrated throughout the Republic of Ireland. In some places, it is primarily a religious event, observed with mass. Parades and smaller celebrations are also typical in many towns. Saint Patrick's Day also marks the beginning of the tourist season and the start of a series of spring, summer, and autumn festivals.

Below: **Saint Patrick's Cathedral in Dublin is the largest church in Ireland and the center of the Protestant Church of Ireland.**

Textiles of Ireland

In seventeenth-century France, Protestants suffered great religious persecution at the hands of the Catholic authorities. In 1685, the French King Louis XIV revoked the only law that guaranteed French Protestant rights, causing about 250,000 Huguenots, or French Protestants, to flee the country. Some of these refugees, many of whom were weavers by profession, came to an area of Northern Ireland called Antrim, bringing their trade with them. At first, weaving was a cottage industry that took place on a small scale. Flax was grown on family farms, and women and children would spin the flax into thread and weave it into fabric. This fabric was sold, unbleached, as brown linen at fairs. Eventually Brown Linen Halls were established as places where drapers (tradespeople who made cloth into clothing, bed linen, and the like) could purchase linen directly from the weavers.

Below: **Wool sweaters are essential in Ireland, where the weather can get very wet and cold.**

In 1764, an Antrim man named William Coulson became the first person in Northern Ireland to produce a fine type of linen called damask. He went on to supply the British, Swedish, and Russian royal families with this delicate fabric. Twenty years later, in 1784, Irish textile workers were introduced to new, labor-saving techniques that involved using water to power the linen twisting machines. In 1823, flax spinning machinery came to Antrim, which then became the home of the largest linen-thread works in the world. Northern Ireland is still famous as a linen-producing region, where high-quality linen sheets, tablecloths, and garments are made. Linen is also produced in the Republic, and hand-embroidered linen is a specialty of textile workers in County Donegal.

Above: **Donegal tweed has set the county of Donegal on the world map.**

Irish Wool

Linen is not the only trademark Irish textile. Irish wool is also popular and well made. Because of Ireland's wet climate, warm clothing has always been essential. Irish wool is made into everything from overcoats to mittens. The two main types of woolen products are knitted goods, such as sweaters, and woven goods, such as blankets and fabric for making clothes. All Ireland's wool is locally produced. Two of the most famous Irish woolens are Donegal tweeds and Aran oiled wool sweaters.

Irish Tweed

Tweed is a textured wool with flecks of color throughout the thread, which accent the overall color of the wool. Donegal tweeds are known for their texture, the tension of the weave, and the subtle colors used to dye the wool. Originally, natural dyes made from minerals, local plants, and lichens were used. Today, most manufacturers prefer synthetic dyes, which are more permanent.

Aran Wool

Aran wool sweaters are famous for their durability and their beautiful knitted designs. The Aran Islands, located off Ireland's western coast, are inhabited by fishermen and farmers who spend a lot of time outdoors, in wet weather. Oiling the wool makes their sweaters water resistant. Each Aran sweater pattern is unique to a family and is handed down from generation to generation.

Vikings in Dublin

In the eighth century, Ireland was populated by Celts most of whom had been Christianized. They did not have a strong central government, so when Viking raiders arrived on Ireland's eastern coast late in the eighth century, they were met with little resistance. The Vikings founded Dublin in 841. They established a settlement and harbor on the banks of the River Liffey, at what is now Wood Quay, and they built a fort where the Rivers Liffey and Poddle met, at a pool on the site of what is now Dublin Castle.

Below: **During the ninth to eleventh centuries, Viking longships cruised the coastal regions of what are now Britain, Ireland, France, and Russia.**

These Norse invaders established trading centers for silver and slaves, using piracy to obtain the "goods" they traded.

In 1014, Brian Boru, a Celt, defeated the Vikings in the Battle of Clontarf, after which the Vikings became fully integrated with the local Irish clans and adopted Christian beliefs. Only about 150 years later, however, this successful Norse-Irish trading community was forced out by the 1170 invasion of Strongbow and his Anglo-Norman soldiers from Britain. This invasion marked the beginning of modern Irish communities and the end of Norse-Irish society.

Rediscovering Dublin's Past

It was not until the 1970s, when Wood Quay was being excavated to lay foundations for large office buildings, that the remains of the Viking settlements around Dublin were discovered. These finds led to clashes between developers, who wanted to build on the site, and conservationists, who wanted to study the site and build a museum there to house their finds. A compromise was reached in which development of the site was postponed while archaeologists carried out excavations and removed what they recovered — an assortment of tools, swords, pottery, coins, leatherwork, combs, brooches, cloak pins, and similar items.

These relics are now on display at the National Museum of Ireland, along with descriptions of how and by whom they were used.

Above: **Vikings in the Norse lands (now Scandinavia) prepare for a raiding expedition.**

A Viking Memorial

The archaeological site of Wood Quay on the River Liffey was eventually developed and is now home to two large civic office buildings, known as "The Bunkers." To commemorate the ancient Viking site, there is a plaque and an unusual picnic site in the shape of a Viking longboat.

RELATIONS WITH NORTH AMERICA

Ireland and North America enjoy a very close friendship. So many Americans claim Irish ancestry that the United States is said to have a larger population of Irish than Ireland itself! This section discusses the political and economic ties between Ireland and North America, as well as some of the major contributions of Irish immigrants to North American culture.

Since the Great Famine of 1845–1848 created large communities of Irish peasants in North America, the United

Opposite: In the 1850s, Cobh Harbour was the main port where Irish emigrants boarded ships bound for the United States. They left to escape miserable conditions in Ireland resulting from the Great Famine. Today, it is a center for sailing and fishing.

States and Canada have, for the most part, extended their support for Irish causes, particularly independence from Britain and "the Troubles" in Northern Ireland.

Today, people of Irish descent contribute to the political, economic, and cultural development of the United States and Canada. North Americans, in turn, introduce many products and services to Ireland, and American and Canadian tourists make up a large proportion of visitors to Ireland every year. Many Irish-Americans visit Ireland to learn more about their Irish roots.

Above: Green is the dominant color during Saint Patrick's Day celebrations in New York City, which has the largest Irish immigrant population in the United States.

Leaving Ireland

Prior to the breakup of the legal union between Britain and Ireland, Ireland's relations with the outside world were almost entirely focused on Britain. Irish immigration to the United States began in earnest in the middle of the nineteenth century. During the Great Famine, in which the potato crop was blighted for a number of years, many people were forced to flee Ireland in the hope of finding food and work in North America, Australia, and Britain. Between the late 1840s and the early 1920s, about four million Irish people left their country.

At the start of the exodus, or mass emigration, from Ireland, more than one million Irish arrived in the United States. By 1850, about 26 percent of New York's population was Irish-born, and, five years later, there were 1.5 million people of Irish birth in the United States. Although the number of Irish emigrants is

Left: **Many Irish immigrants had to endure horrendous conditions in overcrowded ships bound for the United States. Many died from disease and starvation and never made it to the Land of the Free.**

Left: **Early Irish immigrants who arrived in New York were processed through Castle Garden and, later, through Ellis Island. Most made their way either to New York City or to Boston, where large Irish communities had settled. Many of these unskilled immigrants faced difficulties finding work and were forced to endure impoverished living conditions.**

lower today, over one-third of the people born in Ireland live in another country.

Life in the New Land

Most Irish immigrants were poor and had few skills, and they were not always welcome in the countries that received them. In fact, in America and, later, in Britain, advertisements for workers often included the phrase "No Irish Need Apply." Although some immigrants found jobs and eventually became rich, the majority of Irish in America worked in menial jobs. Possibly because they mostly spoke Gaelic and kept to themselves, they did not integrate, or blend in well, with other, better-established immigrant communities.

Today, Irish traditions have become a part of American culture, and many Irish Americans have forged successful careers. According to U.S. census reports, there are currently as many as 44 million people in the United States who claim Irish blood, and approximately 11 million people of pure Irish descent. Many Irish Americans still have ties to Ireland and visit their relatives living there.

Friction with Britain

By the 1860s, there was a large Irish community in America. As dissatisfaction over British rule persisted, an Irish nationalist secret society known as the Fenians continued to press for independence from Britain in Ireland, the United States, and Britain. The Fenian movement was established in Ireland by James Stephens in 1858. Irish immigrant John O'Mahony founded the American Fenians. In 1866, 1870, and 1871, the American Fenians staged unsuccessful uprisings across the American border into British Canada, angering the British government and causing tensions between the United States and Britain.

Consolidating Ties

The Irish found many sympathizers among the Americans, who had themselves fought for independence from Britain in the eighteenth century. Advocates in the United States ranged from ordinary individuals, to powerful politicians with Irish connections, to influential Irish-American lobbying groups.

Below: **Crowds in Dublin gather to watch Fenian prisoners being brought in after the failed Fenian rising of 1866.**

Left: **President John F. Kennedy was one of the most famous Irish-Americans. This picture shows Kennedy visiting his cousin, Mrs. Mary Ryan, in Wexford, Ireland, in 1963.**

In the late 1950s and early 1960s, the presidency of John F. Kennedy, an Irish Catholic, in the United States consolidated, or firmed, relations between the United States and Ireland. When Ireland was accepted into the United Nations in 1955, it was fully recognized as a sovereign nation. Since that time, Ireland and North America have maintained steady, warm relations.

Strong relations between Ireland and North America are also evident in the large number of North American-based businesses with offices in Ireland, as well as in widespread support, both in the United States and in Ireland, for U.S. President Bill Clinton's assistance in the Northern Ireland Peace Talks. Today, the United States remains one of Ireland's principal export markets.

Current Relations

U.S. President Bill Clinton made his first state visit to Ireland in 1995. Although he upset some Protestants in Northern Ireland by shaking hands with Gerry Adams, the leader of Sinn Fein, his visit gave the peace process a massive boost.

President Clinton visited Ireland again in the fall of 1998, showing firm U.S. support for the Good Friday Peace Agreement and its approval by popular vote in both Northern Ireland and in the Republic of Ireland. A group of U.S. senators and representatives has called for a 25 percent increase in U.S. contributions to the International Fund for Ireland, to support the peace agreement.

Economy

North American businesses are moving increasingly into the Irish market. Many have opened plants in the Republic of Ireland, particularly around Dublin and Galway. Leading business people

Below: **U.S. President Bill Clinton (*right*), who has Irish blood, was instrumental in the drafting and signing of the Good Friday Peace Agreement. He is seen here talking with the leader of Sinn Fein, Gerry Adams.**

are now exploring both Northern Ireland and the Republic as potential sites for expanding business relationships between North America and Ireland. American and Canadian companies have expressed support for the peace process and are discussing the possibility of using economic investment incentives to ensure the success of the agreement.

Above: **Large numbers of Irish Americans visit Ireland every year to explore the country and learn about their Irish heritage.**

Tourism

Riding on prosperous economic ties and the large Irish-American presence in the United States, a new wave of tourism has hit Ireland. With relatively inexpensive travel options, North Americans are increasingly attracted to the gorgeous landscapes and rich culture of Ireland. Many also visit the country to rediscover their Irish heritage or to see Irish relatives and ancestral home towns. Tourism has boosted Ireland's economy and, at the same time, raised awareness of Irish issues in North America. There is every indication that this close relationship between Ireland and its North American friends will continue.

Left: Former actress Grace Kelly (*center*), the epitome of style and beauty in the 1950s and 1960s, was of Irish descent. She is seen here with Mrs. (Eamon) de Valera (*far left*) and then-President Sean Lemass (*far right*) at a government reception at Dublin Castle. In 1956, Grace Kelly abandoned a successful Hollywood career to marry Prince Ranier of Monaco. She made regular visits to her family's farmstead in Ireland in the 1960s. In 1982, she died from injuries sustained in a tragic car accident in France.

Irish Americans

Today, the Irish have integrated well into American life. They have formed strong communities in many large cities, including Boston, New York City, San Francisco, and Chicago. These communities have maintained solid relations with Ireland.

Because of the vast numbers who have migrated to the United States, Irish people often feel culturally closer to the United States than they do to European countries that are physically much nearer Ireland. Thus, many young Irish flock to American shores for summer jobs or for permanent residency. Conversely, "ethnic tourism," whereby people of foreign descent return to their original homelands to rediscover their ethnic roots, has become very popular in the United States, bringing many Irish Americans on vacations to Ireland. The revival of interest in Ireland stems in part from the fact that having Irish blood is no longer seen as a stigma (a stain on one's reputation). People who would once have hidden their impoverished roots are increasingly proud of their Irish ancestry. Four prominent U.S. presidents — John F. Kennedy, Richard Nixon, Ronald Reagan, and Bill Clinton — along with many other famous Americans, including former actress Grace Kelly, have Irish ancestors.

North Americans Living in Ireland

Although Ireland does not have a very large rate of immigration, growing numbers of people are moving there to live, work or study Irish art or Celtic history. Still other people travel to Ireland to seek out their Irish roots or simply to retire to the peaceful Irish countryside, away from the hectic world.

The formation of the European Union (EU), to which Ireland belongs, has expanded business and travel opportunities in Europe. Anyone with an Irish-born grandparent can easily get an Irish passport and then work in any European country in the EU without having to obtain a work permit, or the equivalent of a green card. Together, these factors have encouraged many North Americans to consider spending some time in Ireland. Although unemployment in Ireland is relatively high and taxes can be discouraging, the lure of working in a foreign country still brings many enthusiastic North Americans to Irish shores.

Above: **The Irish icons of the leprechaun and the shamrock come together with the American symbol of freedom, the Statue of Liberty, in this cartoon.**

Below: **A bagpipe band plays rousing music in a Saint Patrick's Day parade in New York City.**

Irish Culture

Cultural connections between Ireland and the United States are strong. Irish immigrants to North America brought with them their music, their food, their connection to community, and their skilled craftsmanship. The sheer numbers of Irish immigrants ensured that these cultural influences would be felt and melded into the cultures of North America.

In the United States, perhaps the greatest Irish influence has been felt in the musical arena. Irish musical traditions have contributed to the development of bluegrass, folk, and country music — an influence shown in the work of performers such as Emmylou Harris and Pete Seeger. American musicians have adopted Irish-style melodies and harmonies, methods of storytelling through song, and musical instruments. Irish musicians, such as U2, Enya, and Sinead O'Connor, are also influencing rock and alternative musicians in North America and around the world.

Above: **The Corrs, an Irish family group, is one of today's most popular bands. Recently, they teamed up with the traditional Irish group, the Chieftains, to popularize traditional Irish music.**

Like music, Irish food and beer have made a mark in North America. Irish soda, bread, cheese, and Guinness beer are popular not only in areas with large Irish communities but also elsewhere, and Irish-style pubs are appearing across the North American continent. These bars and restaurants are popular for their spirited atmosphere, good selection of beers, and, often, fabulous music. The Irish would call them places to have some *good craic,* which means "fun."

American Influences

Television, movies, and music have brought the United States and Canada closer to Ireland. North American styles of housing and development have also become popular in Ireland. Eastern Ireland has many wide two- and four-lane highways, large shopping centers, and architecture similar to developments in the United States and Canada. Tourism has deepened the impact of North American culture on Ireland. Many Irish businesses are catering to the expectations of North American visitors. Fast food chains, such as McDonald's, are gaining ground in the Irish economy, and some people see them as a threat to Irish culture. If the spread of Irish traditions all over North America is any indication, however, Irish culture is very much alive and thriving.

Above: **Daniel Day-Lewis is one of Ireland's most accomplished actors. He has starred in several well-known films, including** *In the Name of the Father,* *The Age of Innocence,* **and** *The Boxer.*

Left: **Irish actor Liam Neeson (***front, second from left***) plays Scottish patriot Rob Roy in the acclaimed film of the same name.**

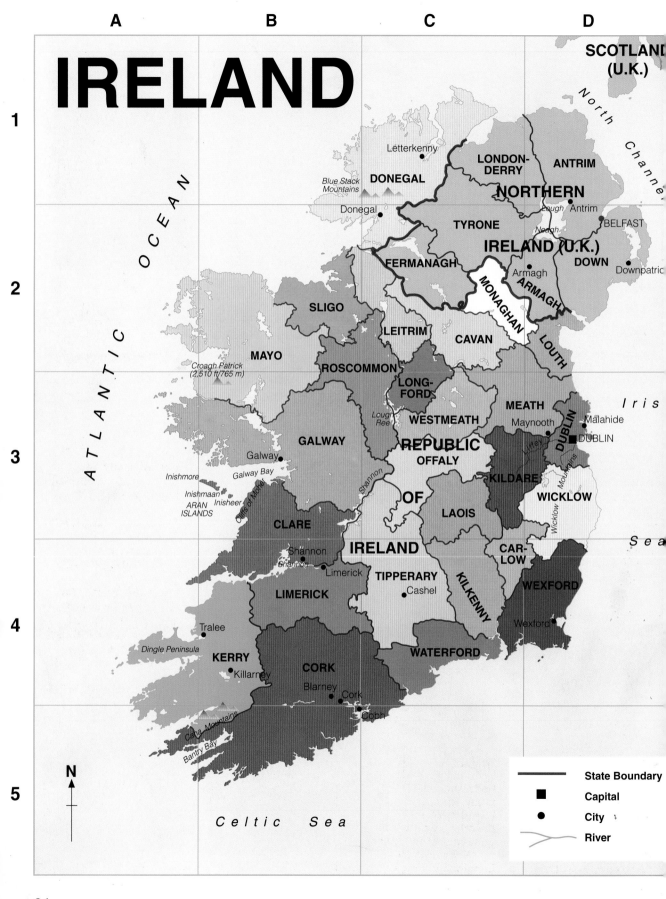

IRELAND

A   B   C   D

SCOTLAND
(U.K.)

North Channel

1

Letterkenny

Blue Stack
Mountains

DONEGAL

LONDON-
DERRY

ANTRIM

NORTHERN

Donegal

TYRONE

Lough
Neagh

Antrim

BELFAST

FERMANAGH

IRELAND (U.K.)

DOWN

ATLANTIC OCEAN

MONAGHAN

Armagh

ARMAGH

Downpatric

2

SLIGO

LEITRIM

CAVAN

LOUTH

MAYO

ROSCOMMON

Iris

Croagh Patrick
(2,510 ft/765 m)

LONG-
FORD

MEATH

Malahide

Lough
Ree

WESTMEATH

Maynooth

DUBLIN

DUBLIN

GALWAY

REPUBLIC

Liffey

Galway

OFFALY

KILDARE

Mountains

3

Inishmore

Galway Bay

OF

WICKLOW

Inishmaan
ARAN
ISLANDS

Inisheer

Cliffs of Moher

LAOIS

Wicklow

Sea

Shannon

CLARE

IRELAND

CAR-
LOW

Shannon

Shannon

Limerick

TIPPERARY

KILKENNY

WEXFORD

LIMERICK

Cashel

Tralee

Wexford

4

Dingle Peninsula

KERRY

CORK

WATERFORD

Killarney

Blarney

Cork

Caha Mountains

Cobh

Bantry Bay

N

5

Celtic Sea

	State Boundary
■	Capital
●	City
~	River

86

Above: These colorful fishing boats are lined up after a hard day's work.

Antrim, city
 (N. Ireland) D1
Antrim, county
 (N. Ireland) D1
Aran Islands B3
Armagh, city
 (N. Ireland) D2
Armagh, county
 (N. Ireland) C2–D2
Atlantic Ocean A1–A5

Bantry Bay B5
Belfast (N. Ireland) D2
Blarney B4
Blue Stack
 Mountains C1

Caha Mountains B4–B5
Carlow, county C4
Cashel C4
Cavan, county C2
Celtic Sea B5
Clare, county B3–B4
Cliffs of Moher B3
Cobh B5
Cork, city B4
Cork, county B4–B5
Croagh Patrick B3

Dingle Peninsula A4
Donegal, city C2
Donegal, county C1

Down, county
 (N. Ireland) D2
Downpatrick D2
Dublin, city D3
Dublin, county D3

Fermanagh, county
 (N. Ireland) C2

Galway, city B3
Galway, county B3
Galway Bay B3

Inisheer B3
Inishmaan B3
Inishmore B3
Irish Sea D3–D4

Kerry, county A4–B4
Kildare, county C3–D3
Kilkenny, county C4
Killarney B4

Laois, county C3
Leitrim, county C2
Letterkenny C1
Liffey, River D3
Limerick, city B4
Limerick, county B4
Londonderry, county
 (N. Ireland) C1
Longford, county C2–C3

Lough Neagh
 (N. Ireland) D2
Lough Ree C3
Louth, county D2

Malahide D3
Maynooth D2
Mayo, county B2–B3
Meath, county C3–D3
Monaghan, county C2

North Channel D1
Northern Ireland C1–D2

Offaly, county C3

Roscommon, county
 B2–C3

Scotland D1
Shannon, city B4
Shannon, River B4–C3
Sligo, county B2

Tipperary, county C3–C4
Tralee B4
Tyrone, county
 (N. Ireland) C1–C2

Waterford, county C4
Westmeath, county C3
Wexford, city C4–D4
Wexford, county D3–D4
Wicklow, county D3
Wicklow Mountains D3

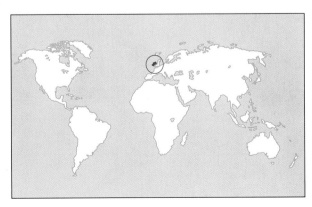

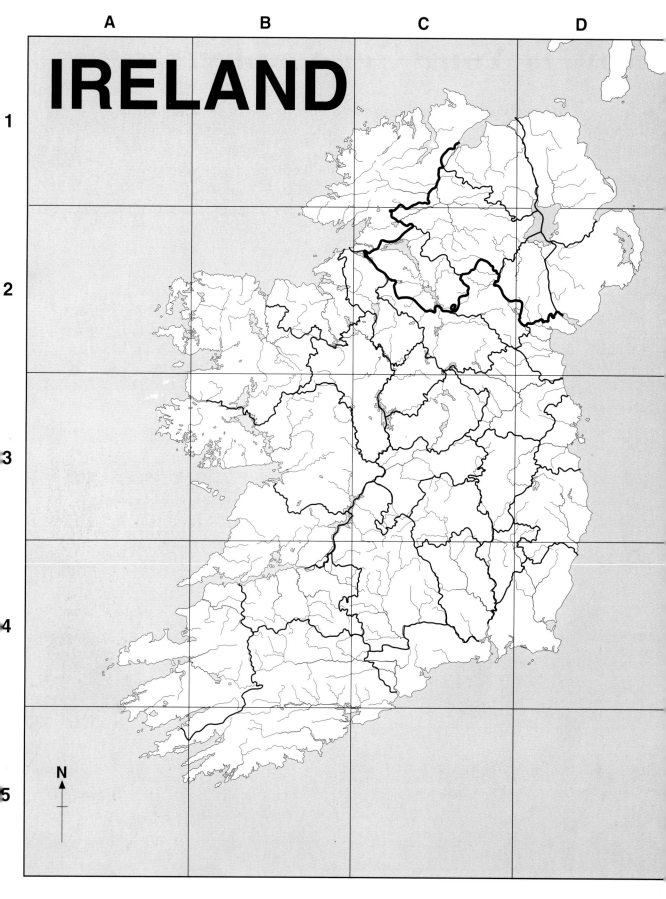

IRELAND

N

How Is Your Geography?

Learning to identify the main geographical areas and points of a country can be challenging. Although it may seem difficult at first to memorize the locations and spellings of major cities or the names of mountain ranges, rivers, deserts, lakes, and other prominent physical features, the end result of this effort can be very rewarding. Places you previously did not know existed will suddenly come to life when referred to in world news, whether in newspapers, television reports, or other books and reference sources. This knowledge will make you feel a bit closer to the rest of the world, with its fascinating variety of cultures and physical geography.

Used in a classroom setting, the instructor can make duplicates of this map using a copy machine. (PLEASE DO NOT WRITE IN THIS BOOK!) Students can then fill in any requested information on their individual map copies. Used one-on-one, the student can also make copies of the map on a copy machine and use them as a study tool. The student can practice identifying place names and geographical features on his or her own.

Below: **These picturesque ruins are Dunluce Castle in Antrim, in Northern Ireland.**

Ireland at a Glance

Official Name The Republic of Ireland (Northern Ireland and Great Britain together make up the United Kingdom)

Capital Dublin (Northern Ireland's capital is Belfast)

Official Languages English and Gaelic

Population 3,539,000 (1998 estimate)

Land Area 27,136 square miles (70,283 square km)

Counties Carlow, Cavan, Clare, Cork, Donegal, Dublin, Galway, Kerry, Kildare, Kilkenny, Laois, Leitrim, Limerick, Longford, Louth, Mayo, Meath, Monaghan, Offaly, Roscommon, Sligo, Tipperary, Waterford, Westmeath, Wexford, Wicklow

Main Rivers River Liffey, River Shannon

Major Lake Lough Ree

Major Mountains Blue Stack Mountains, Caha Mountains

Main Religion Catholicism (Northern Ireland is mainly Protestant)

Famous Leaders Daniel O'Connell, Eamon de Valera, Michael Collins, Mary Robinson, Gerry Adams, Bertie Ahern

Major Festivals Saint Patrick's Day, Easter, Christmas, Saint Stephen's Day

Main Anniversaries Independence from Britain (April 18, 1949)

Easter Rising (Easter Monday, 1916)

National Symbol Harp

National Anthem *The Soldier's Song*

Major Industries Agriculture, manufacturing, finance, industry, tourism

Currency Punt, or Irish pound (IR£0.73 = U.S. $1 as of 1999)

Northern Ireland uses the pound sterling (£0.604 = U.S. $1 as of 1999)

Opposite: **Ivy and beautiful flowers adorn many Irish cottages.**

Glossary

Gaelic Vocabulary

bodhran (BOAR-an): a round, hand-held drum that makes a soft thump when struck with a short wooden drumstick.

boireann (BWIR-ren): rocky land; the rock.

ceilis (KAY-lees): a form of traditional Irish entertainment that combines dancing and music.

Celts (KELTZ): members of a group of western European peoples, including the pre-Roman inhabitants of Britain and Gaul (France) and their descendants, especially in Ireland, Wales, Scotland, and parts of England.

Gaelic (GAY-lik): a Celtic language spoken in Ireland and Scotland; the Irish language.

Taoiseach (TEE-shock): prime minister.

uillean (IL-lee-an) **pipes**: a traditional Irish instrument similar to bagpipes.

English Vocabulary

accord: a signed agreement; a peace accord is a peace agreement, or treaty.

back roads: insignificant tracks, usually found in rural areas.

banshee: a mythical female spirit believed to wail outside houses to signal the death of someone inside.

barrister: in British law, a lawyer with the privilege of attending and arguing in the courts.

bedeviled: continuously plagued, tormented, or harassed.

bethrothal: an engagement; a promise to marry.

blanket bog: rich, organic sediment that has accumulated over thousands of years in large areas fed by moving water.

blight: a plant disease caused by mildews, fungi, or insects.

Bloody Sunday: a violent incident in 1972, in which British soldiers killed thirteen demonstrators in Londonderry, Northern Ireland.

cadence: variation in the pitch of the voice when speaking.

calligraphy: the art of writing elegant script using pen and ink.

cease-fire: a period of truce or suspension of hostilities.

civil wars: wars between people in the same country.

contraception: the intentional prevention of pregnancy.

crenelated: describing stone walls with evenly spaced slits.

crocheted: describing handicrafts made from thread or yarn using interlocking stitches made with a hooked needle.

curriculum: the subjects that are studied or prescribed for study in a school.

deposed: removed from power.

druids: professional learned men who taught the practices and beliefs of a nature-based pagan religion in the early days of Irish history.

elitist: supporting the practice of or belief in the rule or superiority of a certain, usually wealthy, class.

emancipation: freedom from bondage.

embellished: richly decorated.

émigrés: emigrants; people who leave their homelands to live in other countries.

extorted: obtained something, usually money, from a person by force, violence, or the abuse of power.

facilitate: to help or enable; to make easier.

fry: a large traditional Irish breakfast, consisting of fried eggs, bacon or sausages, grilled tomatoes, brown bread, and black or white pudding.

hierarchical: describing a system in which grades or classes of status or authority are ranked one above the other.

homosexuality: sexual attraction to members of the same gender.

Huguenots: seventeenth-century French Protestants who were persecuted for their faith by French Catholic authorities.

influx: a flowing in of people, things, or ideas.

innovative: inventive; creative.

integrated: describing the combination of many parts into a whole.

leprechauns: small, mischievous people of Irish folklore. Leprechauns were said to possess pots of gold.

lyrical: describing literature, usually poetry, that expresses the writer's emotions in certain recognized forms.

machicolations: high, projecting walls from which weapons may be launched.

metropolitan: describing a region made up of a large, central city surrounded by smaller communities.

monogram: a design usually consisting of two or more combined alphabetic letters, such as a person's initials.

pagans: persons not subscribing to any of the major religions of the world.

peat: rich, organic matter that is removed from bogs and used primarily for fuel and fertilizer; also called *turf*.

Penal Laws: a set of laws imposed on Catholics in the sixteenth and seventeenth centuries by Protestants in Britain and Ireland. These laws, enforced primarily in the seventeenth century, removed social rights from Catholics, including the right to own or lease land.

promontory: a piece of land that juts high above a body of water or over an expanse of land.

provocative: tending to arouse emotions or prompt action.

retract: to withdraw; to take back.

revoked: withdrew; retracted.

rife: teeming; abounding.

scribes: persons who handwrite documents, especially ancient or medieval manuscript copyists.

secularization: the process of change by which something becomes less and less bound by religious rules and influences.

shamrock: a plant with three leaves on a single stem; the national emblem of Ireland.

surmounted: overcame.

Vikings: Norse explorers and pirates who sailed the seas of Europe in longships between the ninth and eleventh centuries, raiding existing villages and setting up their own settlements in Ireland, Britain, and parts of what are now France and Russia.

Winter Solstice: December 21, the shortest day in the year, when the sun reaches its lowest point in the sky at noon.

More Books to Read

Celtic Myths and Legends. Eoin Neeson (Irish Amer Book Company)

Cooking the Irish Way. Helga Hughes (Lerner Publications Company)

Dublin. Cities of the World series. Deborah Kent (Children's Press)

The Famine Secret. Cora Harrison (Irish Amer Book Company)

Favorite Irish Folktales. Seamus MacManus (Dover)

The Heartbeat of Irish Music. Christy McNamara and Peter Woods (Roberts Rinehart)

The History of Emigration from Ireland. Origins series. Katherine Prior (Frankin Watts)

Ireland. Festivals of the World series. Patricia McKay (Gareth Stevens)

Ireland. Land of the Poets series. David Lyons (Thunder Bay Press)

Mary Robinson: A Woman of Ireland and the World. John Horgan (Roberts Rinehart)

Northern Ireland: Troubled Land. World in Conflict series. Eric Black (Lerner)

Saint Patrick: A Visual Celebration. Courtney Davis (Blandford)

Videos

Beauty of Ireland. (Global Sourcing)

Ireland: Western Ireland, Dublin, and Belfast. (Questar)

Legends of Ireland: Fairies and Leprechauns. (Acorn Media)

Out of Ireland: The Story of Emigration into America. (Shanachie Video)

Web Sites

www.ireland.com/

www.iftn.ie/index.html

www.globalirish.com/dir/politics.html

www.ireland-now.com/castles/index.html

Due to the dynamic nature of the Internet, some web sites stay current longer than others. To find additional web sites, use a reliable search engine with one or more of the following keywords to help you locate information about Ireland. Keywords: *Celts, Dublin, Ireland, Irish music, James Joyce, Northern Ireland, Saint Patrick, shamrock.*

Index